CONVERSATIONS WITH LUKÁCS

Conversations with Lukács

Hans Heinz Holz
Leo Kofler
Wolfgang Abendroth

Edited by Theo Pinkus

The MIT Press
Cambridge, Massachusetts

© Rowohlt Verlag 1967, Merlin Press 1974
First published in the English language
by the Merlin Press Ltd., London

First MIT Press edition, 1975

Library of Congress Cataloging in Publication Data

Lukács, György, 1885-1971.
 Conversations with Lukács.

 Translation of Gespräche mit Georg Lukács.
 I. Holz, Hans Heinz. II. Pinkus, Theodor,
 1909-   ed. III. Title.
 B4815.L84A513 1975   199'.439   74-34021
 ISBN 0-262-16062-5

Contents

Foreword   7

First Conversation
  Being and Consciousness   13

Second Conversation
  Society and the Individual   41

Third Conversation
  Elements for a Scientific Politics   81

Fourth Conversation
  Provisional Summary   119

Foreword

Georg Lukács is one of the most influential thinkers of our century, and this influence extends over different periods of his activity. It commences with his early *Soul and Form*, inspired by the philosophy of vitalism, in which Lukács had not yet renounced the heritage of Simmel; this work belonged to that time of ferment in Germany, still unclear in its social direction, of which expressionism is the characteristic product. Then came the first major testimony of Marxist philosophy of history, *History and Class Consciousness*, a work which left its mark on a whole generation of young European intellectuals. Finally, after World War Two, Lukács produced the polemical analyses of *The Destruction of Reason*, and other writings on literary history in the same vein, in which he developed, starting from the principles of rationality and enlightenment, a progressive and militant position against the irrationalism and obscurantism of late bourgeois ideology. The fertility of Lukács's influence does not lie only in the methods and insights that he has produced, but perhaps still more in the way he provokes opposition, and forces his opponents to clarify their own positions, so that even in their rebuttals, where these proceed on the pertinent level of the argument, something of the lucidity of Lukács's thought is necessarily reflected.

Lukács is a committed thinker. It is part of his style that his thought is aroused by the concrete case, by the occasion at hand. The majority of his works are therefore specific investigations, forming a kind of circle around a common centre. It was only at an advanced age that Lukács could make this centre, the philosophical kernel of his work, the express object of his consideration. His complete philosophy is still outstanding; its first component is the two-volume first part of the *Aesthetic*, and an *Ontology* is next in line.

It was the idea of the editor of the present volume that it would be helpful for the reader of Lukács's writings to direct some initial and provisional probes into this centre, where his conceptions are rooted and founded. We should encroach, so to speak, on the scholar's production process, in order to facilitate the approach to his many-sided work, and to open it up to a broader readership. The form of conversation presented itself as one in which weighty considerations and deductions would be abridged to simpler formulations. Conversations recorded on tape would be less of a burden to a man more than eighty years old, and would impede his progress on his own major work less than a short written introduction to his basic positions. It was therefore suggested that Lukács might discuss with three interlocutors questions of ontology, politics and ideological criticism, in such a way as to show the internal connection of the principal elements of his creative work.

The conversational form offered the further advantage of maintaining the animated expression which is inevitably lost in the transition from speech to the written word. Lukács is Hungarian, and his verbal expression, when unrestrained, results in an impetuous and temperamental German which is by no means free from error. When he writes, this flood of language is smoothed over and replaced by sentences of complex classical construction, the style acquires the gestures of scientific demonstration—and part of that free and easy spontaneity of verbal expression gets lost. Each of us has the same experience when speaking and writing in our own mother tongue. Conversation would preserve the freshness of formulation and show how a thought first emerges and how its strands of meaning, gradually broadening out, are then again joined together and referred back to their starting-point. The goal was not precision of treatment, but rather the documentary value of the original presentation. There were also to be no polemics, but a common investigation of the matters involved.

Lukács is a fulminating speaker. A small stimulus, the fragment of an idea, is sufficient to set in motion his own train of thought and association. Fuelled as this is by a wealth of knowledge born of experience, once started, it can no longer be restrained. Anyone who speaks with him must be above all a good listener. We sat in his spacious apartment on the Danube embankment, at a table covered with drinks and pastries, with a view of the river and the citadel on the other side; behind us the walls were lined with books, right up to the ceiling of the high room. A scholar's apartment, in a style thoroughly appropriate to the old atmosphere of the Austro-Hungarian empire which even today still marks the face of Budapest, however different the contents which now fill these 'external forms'. The people of this city have a *savoir-vivre*, an urbane politeness, a generous *liberté*—and it is no accident that it is in French descriptions that this characterization occurs. There is an elective affinity between Budapest and Paris, which even shows itself in the thought and speech of Lukács: his thought is marked by irony and *ésprit*, averse to any kind of melancholy which fishes in troubled waters, and dominated by the Cartesian commandment of clarity and distinctness, for which any true statement, however trivial, is preferable to the highest—but unfoundable—effulgences of mysticism.

Lukács thus allows no obscurities. It is certainly not by chance that, out of all the neo-positivists whom he attacks so forcibly, he acknowledges only Wittgenstein as a really significant philosopher, Wittgenstein who said, 'The correct method in philosophy would really be the following: to say nothing except what can be said, i.e. propositions of natural science—i.e. something that has nothing to do with philosophy—and then, whenever someone else wanted to say something metaphysical, to demonstrate to him that he had failed to give a meaning to certain signs in his propositions.' This elimination of every kind of metaphysics is exactly in Lukács's own spirit—and it is characteristic of what he calls 'ontology' (and he returned to this again and again in our conversations) that it can be expressed in completely unmetaphysical statements. Only under this condition is it permissible and meaningful to reinstate the term and subject of 'ontology'.

There is thus a basic empiricism in Lukács's thought, which comes through more directly in conversation than in the high-level abstractions of theoretical formulation. These conversations show very clearly the basis of abstraction in the experiences of everyday life. The data provided by everyday intercourse with the real world will play an essential and methodologically decisive role in Lukács's *Ontology*, as they have already done in his *Aesthetic*. This gives these conversations with Lukács a more than anecdotal value; for the unmediated way in which thought is produced in conversation corresponds exactly to that primary level of experience, the data of everyday reality, whose theoretical relevance Lukács emphasizes.

In transcribing the conversations, it was therefore our aim to retain as far as was possible the impression of the spoken word. On the other hand, it was impossible to avoid smoothing out Lukács's very effervescent speech, which ranged far afield, often without full stops or commas, and fitting it together syntactically in order to make it readable. Something that is quite unambiguous to the listener in live delivery can be confusing for the reader in the neutrality of the printed word. Nevertheless the editorial preparation of the text had to take care not to sacrifice the specific characteristics of Lukács's speech: the long phrasing of the sentences, the effervescent train of thought, the tissue of digression and the return to the basic theme, the far-ranging bearing of the totality. Lukács's empiricism, which we mentioned above, is by no means undialectical. There is a wealth of linguistic evidence of this: long and convoluted sentences, which seek to grasp their object not from one side only, but from several aspects; ancillary clauses with '*wobei*' [in which connection], which supplement the positive formulation of an idea with the negations of its limitation, modification and relativity. (These complex sentences often had to be broken up in transcription.) Lukács also counterposes contrary elements of a single question, which are signalled by the use of 'on the one hand . . . on the other hand', and he articulates an idea with punctuation marks which simultaneously separate and connect, particularly colons and dashes. Such peculiarities of style indicate that Lukács's train of thought, while seeming to drive forward so audaciously, in fact continually assures itself of the many-sided richness of reality. While fixing the goal firmly in its sights, it also looks always to left and right, forwards and back, and so pays attention to the mediation of the totality by the particular, which is of the essence of the dialectical method.

These conversations pursue both a documentary and a propadeutic design. They aspire to bear witness to the living thought of one of the great men of our century, and to provide the opportunity to approach this thought by the simplest possible route. We are grateful to Georg Lukács for submitting to the exertions of these lengthy conversations, on four consecutive days and with untiring *élan*, and for checking the edited manuscript once again before publication. Lukács was for us a shrewd collocutor, a charming host and a friend to whom we are heartily indebted. To listen to him 'is both an honour and a profit'.

Wolfgang Abendroth
Hans Heinz Holz
Leo Kofler
Theo Pinkus

Georg Lukács—Hans Heinz Holz

Being and Consciousness

Holz: Herr Lukács, in your *Aesthetic* you make use of a set of ontological assumptions which are not always and not in all places explicitly discussed. Now we know of course that you are working at an *Ontology* on a Marxist basis, and we do not want to criticize this book, which we have still to read. However we would like to touch a little on one problem, i.e. how certain positions in your *Aesthetic* are conditional on ontological assumptions and will be settled by these. We can perhaps clarify these assumptions somewhat in this conversation. One preliminary question follows from this, which I might perhaps begin with, a question that is particularly important for me at the present time, as it was raised in a discussion which I had in Marburg with students of Herr Abendroth, who is now sitting here beside us.

Is there really any such thing as a Marxist ontology? What meaning can the word 'ontology' have in a Marxist philosophy? This circle of Herr Abendroth's students raised the objection to me that Marxism reduces ontology to sociology. Ontological categories have to be understood simply as social and historical categories. But if ontology is to have any meaning of its own, then these ontological categories must grasp something which cannot be defined purely in social or historical terms. I would be interested to know how you would reply to this question.

Lukács: I would say that whatever you are doing, as a scientist or anything else, you always start out from problems of everyday life, and ontological problems are raised here on a very massive scale. I would like to start with something very simple. Someone is crossing the road. He might be the most obstinate neo-positivist in his epistemology, denying all reality, but he will nevertheless be convinced at the pedestrian crossing that, if he does not remain where he is, he will really be run over by a real car, rather than some kind of mathematical formula of his existence being run over by the mathematical function of the car, or his idea by the idea of the car. I have deliberately taken such a brutally simple example in order to show that in our actual life various different forms of being always converge, and that the relationship of these forms of being is the primary thing. I cannot therefore accept it as a really serious question whether some category or other is sociological or ontological. We have become accustomed to conceiving any kind of discipline that has been academically enfranchised as an independent sphere of being. Even such an astute philosopher as Nicholai Hartmann once argued that the psyche must be an autonomous entity because psychology had been treated in the universities for two or three hundred years as a separate science. Now I am of the opinion that all these things are historically variable, whereas being and its transformations are in this respect fundamental. One must in my opinion take this as the starting-point, which is what I did in my *Aesthetic*. In fact the title 'Specificity of the Aesthetic' is perhaps not quite correct; it would be more accurate to say, the place of the aesthetic principle in the framework of human mental activities.

Now these human mental activities are not, as it were, spiritual entities, as they appear to the university philosophers, but rather various forms in which men organize those actions and reactions of the external world, to which they are always exposed, in some kind of way that will enable them to protect and develop their own existence. Today, for example, it is almost certain that the exquisite Old Stone Age paintings found in the South of France and in Spain were really magical preparations for hunting: that these animals were not painted just for aesthetic reasons, but because the men of that time had the idea that a good likeness of an animal meant that the animal could be more successfully hunted. Painting is here still primarily a utilitarian reaction to life, and as human society becomes more socialized painting progresses with it, so that the immediate reproduction of life is already always conditioned in this way. I would like to say something else very simple now: you go into a shop and buy a tie or half-a-dozen handkerchiefs; if you imagine the process which was necessary for you and the handkerchiefs to meet one another on the market, you might arrive at a very involved, very complicated picture, and I believe that these processes cannot be excluded from an understanding of society. That is the first point which I would like to mention here.

The second point is a methodological one, and in a certain sense it leads already much further. Developed science has a tendency to comprehend every form of life, every living phenomenon, in the highest forms in which it is found, and believes that this is the way to obtain the best analysis. Consider Kant's theory of knowledge, which on the one hand seeks a foundation for knowledge in the mathematics of his time and in Newtonian physics, and on the other hand takes the highly developed moral decision as the basis of practical life. Now I believe that it is impossible to derive the lower form from this higher form. One cannot proceed from the Newtonian form of analysis, from Newtonian physics, to the ideas with which a primitive hunter determined, from the noise it made, whether a stag or a roe deer was nearby. And if I start from the categorical imperative, I will not be able to understand the simple practical behaviour of people in everyday life. I believe therefore that we must follow the genetically determined path, and here we are already in the thick of ontological problems. In other words, we must attempt to investigate conditions in their original forms of appearance, and to see under what conditions these forms of appearance become ever more complicated, ever more mediated.

This is naturally in a certain sense unpleasant for the scientist to hear. If I consider science as an established fact, then this fact of science must have developed from something. In any teleological project, such as labour, there is a moment at which the labouring man—a Stone Age man for example—considers whether a certain instrument is suitable or unsuitable for the purpose he has in mind. If I go back to the time before instruments of labour were produced, and consider the time when primitive man simply selected stones to fulfil certain functions, I can imagine him investigating two stones and saying—whether he actually formulated it as I am doing now or not is quite immaterial—this stone is suitable to cut up a branch, that stone is not suitable. Science begins with this primitive selection of stones. What has happened since is simply that science has gradually developed into an independent apparatus of mediation, so that the paths which lead to the final practical decisions are extraordinarily long, as we can indeed observe today in any factory. And I believe that it is much safer to trace the genesis of science starting from the selection of stones for primitive labour and ending with developed science, than to begin with higher mathematics and then attempt to make one's way back to the selection of stones. That is to say, if I want to understand phenomena genetically, then the path of ontology is completely unavoidable, and the problem is to pick out, in the midst of the many contingencies which accompany the genesis of any phenomenon, the typical moments, those necessary for the process itself. That is certainly the basic reason why I regard the ontological question as the essential one; from an ontological point of view, the precise boundaries drawn between the sciences play a secondary role.

I return once again to my earlier example: if a car comes towards me at a pedestrian crossing, I can conceive the car as a technological phenomenon, as a sociological phenomenon, as a phenomenon of cultural philosophy, etc., but the real car is the unity that either will or will not run me over. The car as a sociological or cultural-philosophical object only results from a mode of consideration which is connected with real features of the car and is the reproduction in thought of these real features, but the existing car is, so to speak, more primary than, let us say, the sociological view of it, for the car will drive on whether I consider it sociologically or not, whereas the sociology of the car will never set any car in motion. Reality thus has an intrinsic order of priority, if I may put it this way, and we should attempt to return to these primitive facts of life, as I consider them, and comprehend the complicated on the basis of the primitive.

Holz: So the starting-point of everyday life is the basis, as it were, a kind of natural understanding of the world. Dilthey or Husserl already used this term, though of course in a different sense to that in which you are using it now.

Lukács: It has also been used in teleological conceptions . . .

Holz: Yes, but the question now is whether ontology, if it must certainly begin genetically in everyday life, does not have, none the less, a specific methodological form with which it approaches the data of this everyday experience and translates them, so to speak, into a system of understanding. The question is, in other words, what is the object of ontology, in this narrower sense? In classical ontology, for example, one would say it was the theory of categories.

Lukács: I would say that its object was the really existing. And its task is to investigate the existing and trace it back to its being, and thus to discover the various gradations and connections contained within it. A point naturally arises here which evidently leads somewhat further, but which I believe it necessary to introduce right at the beginning. This is a problem which, to the best of my knowledge, was first brought into modern discussion by Nikolai Hartmann—the fact, which he perceived already in inorganic nature, that the primary form of existence is the complex, that one must therefore investigate the complex as complex, and proceed from the complex to its elements and elementary processes, and not (as science generally believes), first find certain elements and then construct definite complexes from the interplay of the elements. You will remember that Hartmann conceived the solar system on the one hand, and the atom on the other, as complexes of this kind. I regard this as a very fruitful idea. It is clear without any further consideration that we cannot have any science of biology unless we understand life as something which is primarily complex, in which the life of the whole organism is the ultimate determining force of the particular processes. We could never understand an organism as the synthesis of all its muscular, nervous and other movements —even if we understood each of these individual movements with scientific exactness; rather, these partial processes are only understandable as partial processes of the complex organism.

We now come to our own concern, that is to human society, where this complexity is obviously not only a characteristic of the whole society, but also of the social atom. Man himself is a complex, a complex in the biological sense; social phenomena cannot be understood by decomposing this complex man, and so society must be conceived, from the start, as a complex made up of complexes. Now the decisive question is precisely how these complexes are created and how we can arrive at the real nature of their being and their function. As we have already said, the question is not their sociological and other determinations, which always come later, but how to comprehend genetically the rise and formation of these complexes.

If you consider society from this standpoint, then the one fact for which there is no kind of analogy in the organic world is labour. Labour is, so to speak, the very atom of society (I say this in quotation marks), and is an extraordinarily complicated complex, in which a causal series is set in motion by a teleological project of the labourer. Labour can only be successful if it is a *real* causal series that is set in motion, and indeed, in the direction that the teleological project requires. On the other hand, if I investigate a complex, I come to the fact that the teleological project involved in labour can never take account of the entire set of conditions of the causal series set in motion, so that something must necessarily emerge in the labour process other than what the labourer set himself as his aim. Naturally, at certain primitive stages the deviation might be quite minimal, but it is quite certain that the whole of human development depends on such minimal displacements. Let us say that men found by pure chance the possibility of a better way of sharpening stones. They then gradually came to recognize this as better, and by degrees it became general practice. Progress in general is unimaginable without such a development, in which, as a result of ignorance of the conditions of labour, something always emerges that was not originally envisaged—more exactly, something *else* emerges.

It is a prejudice stemming from scientism to believe that with the increase and collection of experience, the terrain of the unknown diminishes. I believe that it increases. As we get to know nature better, by the action of science and labour, this unknown medium becomes ever more blatant, and has the most important consequences for future human development. This unknown, uncontrolled area of social reproduction is not confined to primitive stages, but exists also at developed ones. You understand how this is related to the ontological question of the construction of the complex. The individual factory owner controls his individual production better than the small handicraftsman of ancient or medieval times, but despite this, the complexity of production and consumption generates the unknown forces which are unleashed in economic crises. I maintain that it is a contemporary prejudice of economic science to believe that Keynes and others have brought the economy under complete control. Those very problems which are so important at the present time, with the end of the German economic miracle, show how impermanent is this control of the economic process.

I now come once again to an ontological question: the higher the degree of complexity of a thing, the more human consciousness is confronted by an extensively and intensively infinite object, and its best knowledge can only be relatively approximate. If I recognize X and Y as properties of an object, there is still no guarantee that Z and other properties are not also present, and under certain conditions will not become practically effective. I believe that we can come to grips with these facts only in the form of an ontology, which is concerned with ontological relationships and where we completely set aside whether a certain ontological relationship is treated by present-day science as psychological or sociological or epistemological or logical. We treat this relationship as an existing relationship, and the question of which science is to deal with it is a secondary one. That is in my opinion the essential standpoint of Marxism, and I can appeal here to Marx's celebrated definition that for him, categories, forms of existence or existential determinations, are the direct opposite of, for example, the Kantian and even the Hegelian conception of categories. And you can see at once how the genetic method follows from this if you take the beginning of *Capital*, which does not start with labour but with the most primitive form of commodity exchange. The ontology of commodity exchange leads by way of conclusion to the genetic derivation of money as the universal commodity. Marx then shows how the fact that gold and silver in time became money is in turn ontologically connected with the physical properties of gold and silver. These properties corresponded to the conditions of a generalized exchange, and hence gold and silver everywhere became predominant as the general means of exchange, as money. The fact that money became a mystical power for civilized antiquity, which Marx repeatedly points out, shows how this is the realistic approach to knowledge. Ontologically, money arose in this simple way from acts of exchange, but since the ancients were not yet able to hit on this ontological explanation, you find from Homer and Sophocles onwards, constant laments about a mythical power which has invaded society and usurped domination over men, although it is simply a dead material. Thus a problem which was incomprehensible for entire epochs, became completely clear through the ontological derivation that Marx gives in the beginning of *Capital*. The same goes for another problem, one that even such a significant economist as Ricardo could not solve, i.e. that on the one hand, commodities exchange on the basis of their labour value, while on the other hand, there is in capitalist society an average rate of profit. I believe that Ricardo was aware of this unresolved contradiction between average rate of profit and labour value. Now Marx established the simple fact of social ontology that Ricardo was most probably also aware of, that in modern capitalism capital moves from one area to another. This movement, which in pre-capitalist societies and even in the earliest forms of capitalism is very restricted in its extent, is a basic ontological fact. I mean here again an existential fact of developed capitalism. Now, if you look up Marx's presentation in volume III of *Capital*, you will see that the derivation of profit and average profit from labour value is a simple result of the movement of capital; the great riddle is solved, the moment that we find the correct ontological approach.

We are using the fine word 'ontology', and I have even got into the habit of this, although one should really say that one is discovering the forms of being that new movements of the complex produce. The fact that new phenomena can be genetically derived on the basis of their everyday existence is only one aspect of a general relationship, namely that being is a historical process. There is certainly no Being in the strong sense, and even that which we call everyday being is a specific and extremely relative configuration of complexes within a historical process. Indeed, Marx wrote in *The German Ideology* that there was only a single science, the science of history, and you will remember how enthusiastically Marx greeted Darwin, despite many methodological reservations, for discovering the fundamentally historical character of being in organic nature. As for inorganic nature, it is naturally extremely difficult to establish its historicity. But although I am myself a dilettante in questions of natural science, I believe nevertheless that we are standing on the eve of a really great philosophic revolution brought about through the natural sciences, particularly insofar as atomic physics is beginning to be applied to the observations of astronomy. There are now preliminary indications that the laws of combination of matter which produce complexes such as the sun, for example, are not identical throughout the universe. In different types of stars, different forms of combination of matter have already been found. I do not consider it out of the question that science will someday produce a history of the combination of matter, as a result of which the eternal form of matter, which was the great revolutionary principle of the time of Galileo and Newton, will be shown to be an epoch or a period in the historical development of its structure. I say that now purely in passing, as an expression of my philosophical aspiration, so to speak, for I am an absolute dilettante in this field. Nevertheless Goethe and Lamarck were already attempting to work in this direction, while for the eighteenth century, and still for Cuvier, a historical conception of the development of inorganic nature seemed out of the question. The problem therefore is whether present-day physics is to be based on a so to speak obsolete standpoint—either that of vulgar materialism, or the purely manipulative conception of neo-positivism—or whether we are moving towards a historic and genetic conception of inorganic nature. And in this case Marx's saying—that there is just the one single science of history, from astronomy through to so-called sociology—will turn turn out to be true, as a basic fact of being, which certainly does not prevent the structure of being having three great underlying forms: the inorganic, the organic, and the social.

These three forms are distinguished from one another by qualitative leaps. Nowhere in the inorganic realm is there anything like a periodic reproduction of individual organisms, persisting through fluctuations, any more than there is in the organic world anything analogous to human society—what is called animal society is a complicated question. In any case, human society is a new and specific kind of being. But we should not conceive these leaps in anthropomorphic terms, as if I leap up from the table and run to the telephone. Such a leap can take millions of years, with the most varied advances, regressions, and so on, and it is, I believe, established beyond doubt that among the higher animals there were various advances in the direction of human society, which only led to a real transition with that species of ape from which *homo sapiens* was gradually formed. It follows naturally that one must conceive the relationship between the different spheres in a similarly genetic sense.

A further fact of ontology enters in here, which in my opinion is particularly neglected by the modern sciences. As science develops, the particular sciences establish ever more precise, mathematically formulated relationships within their own areas. This produces a tendency for human thought to consider the accidental as a sort of not-yet-knowledge, which will be ever further eliminated by the improvement of knowledge. If I raise the ontological question of the genesis of the organism (and I can only do so scientifically), present-day discoveries by Oparin, Bernal and others demonstrate the intervention of a fact that in the cosmic sense is accidental, i.e. that at a certain stage in the Earth's cooling, atmospheric pressure, the chemical combination of earth and water, etc. effected by chance the transformation of inorganic matter into organic. The genesis of life is only explicable as a remarkable accident; it cannot be explained purely in terms of the elements involved, but depends on the coincidence of the intrinsically heterogenous series of developments. That is an aspect of things that must be emphasized, because human thinking has supposed that the existence of rationality and lawfulness involves an ontological domination of rationality, while in reality, if I may put it this way, there is only an 'if-then' necessity. Unlimited, absolute necessity is a fantasy of the professors; in my opinion, there is no such thing. History is full of these 'if-then' necessities, and so it is by no means certain how many planets there are in the world, in the universe, on which this kind of chance has brought life into being. And naturally, still further accidents are necessary if, as in our case, a species of ape is to develop with the capacity for labour. Here also, accident plays an extraordinarily great role, and this role of accident, with all its historical consequences, follows from the historicity of the ontological conception of development (in which being is transformed into a process).

Let us return once again to an observation of Marx's. You will remember that Marx once wrote to Kugelmann, with respect to the Paris Commune, that history would be very simple if there were no accidents, and he considered as accidental, for example, the quality of the men who head the workers' movement at any particular time. It is thus quite impossible, in other words, to deduce from the development of the workers' movement the quality of its leaders, since an insuperable element of chance also persists here. I would like to stop here for the time being, so that you see that the introduction of ontology in no way simplifies problems, but on the contrary provides a scientific and philosophical basis for understanding processes in their complexity and hence their rationality. By rationality I always mean 'if-then' rationality. In this way ontology can resolve problems which were previously insoluble, because of the division of labour between the specific scientific disciplines. Didn't Kelsen contend in the 1920s, for example, that the formation of law was a mystery for legal science? Now it is obvious that the formation of law is not at all mysterious. There are the most complicated debates and class struggles around it. The average trader in the Federal Republic will certainly not see it as a mystery, but rather ask himself whether his particular pressure group can exert a sufficiently strong, therefore *de facto* ontological pressure on the government, for a paragraph to be formulated in its interest. Kelsen, however, was not simply a fool to see a mystery here; this follows, rather, precisely from the impossibility of solving problems of real life by logic or epistemology. Logic and epistemology can be good instruments when used critically, in certain circumstances. In and for themselves, however, and where, as in Kantianism, positivism and neo-positivism, questions of epistemology are erected into the main method, they become a hindrance to real knowledge. It is one of the limitations of Hegelian philosophy that it drives a chasm between philosophy and science, while in Marxism science really facilitates, time and again, the solution of ontological questions, as for example that problem of astronomy which we referred to earlier. On the other hand philosophy can apply an ontological criticism to certain scientific presuppositions or theories, by proving that they contradict the factual structure of reality.

Holz: In reply to the question whether a Marxist ontology is possible, you have given me a sketch of one already worked out. In other words, you have answered the question by showing what form such an ontology must assume. Some quite key points now seem to have been mentioned, which we should hang on to in our set of questions.

You said that everything primary in the world consists of phenomena which are complex in nature, and referred on this point to Nikolai Hartmann. The basic question of ontology would then be how these complexes are constituted. Let me put it this way. Ontology regulates each of the sciences as a kind of basic science, so to speak, and can thus intervene in the lacunae between the scientific disciplines and play a mediating function between them.

Lukács: Yes.

Holz: Now according to the Marxist conception—and this seems to me essential—this basic science is always a historical one. You quoted Marx's formulation to the effect that only history functions as a unitary science in the Marxist sense . . .

Lukács: Yes.

Holz: . . . and referred to Darwinism, then to Goethe and Lamarck, to exemplify this problem with the aid of the natural sciences. I might perhaps just add to this in parentheses that the historical conception of nature is already present in certain philosophical positions of the Enlightenment . . .

Lukács: Of course . . .

Holz: . . . and Leibniz's *Protogea* is also an attempt at a historical treatment of earthly nature . . .

Lukács: Of course . . .

Holz: Perhaps one could consider the entire object of the doctrine of monads precisely as a speculative attempt to understand and interpret atomism historically.

Lukács: Yes. If I might put in a comment here, I believe that the study of Leibniz is one of the great omissions of Marxism. Leibniz is an extraordinarily complicated and interesting figure, whom we—I must include myself too in the ranks of sinners— have not yet made any attempt to understand. I agree completely with you about this. It is a task whose results we can in no way anticipate.

Holz: You have really read my thoughts, for Leibniz is at this very moment my own immediate field of work.

Lukács: Very interesting.

Holz: And I might recall that Marx esteemed Leibniz very highly. . .

Lukács: Of course . . .

Holz: . . . and stressed this continually. Lenin's annotations to Feuerbach's book on Leibniz—which by the way is by far the best that has ever been written on Leibniz in German philosophy . . .

Lukács: Feuerbach's book . . .

Holz: . . . Feuerbach's book and Lenin's annotations . . .

Lukács: . . . is very intelligent . . .

Holz: . . . are quite essential for the interpretation of the pre-Hegelian dialectic. But that is simply in passing. We started from the point that ontology, as a basic science, develops certain conceptual models—I use the term 'model' not in the neo-positivist sense, but in a quite general one—and these models establish the relationship of the knowledge of the nature of being produced by the individual sciences.

Lukács: Yes . . .

Holz: We have now come closer to the aesthetic problem again, for the work of art is certainly also the draft of a model, on a narrower scale, insofar as a specific little world is created in each particular work of art.

Lukács: Yes, of course.

Holz: In other words, every work of art has properly, if you like, an ontological intention . . .

Lukács: Yes . . .

Holz: . . . which is to create a possible world, to use once again an expression of Leibniz's . . .

Lukács: Yes . . .

Holz: . . . and thus proceeds from the ontological premise that, in the first instance, the whole world is organized and not chaotic. Modern physics certainly does not leave this premise completely unquestioned, but the work of art, which can only

26

regard as a world an internally ordered system of meanings, thus presupposes that what is developed in the work of art is a cosmos in itself, and that within this closed cosmos all parts are related by more or less necessary connections, or at least in a contingency required by necessity. Now this could mean that any formal system whatsoever, which comprises a closed totality of connections, could be treated by us as a work of art. However we do not do this in ordinary language, nor in the narrow aesthetic sense do we treat any formal system whatsoever as a work of art. If we speak of a work of art, we mean rather that the little world which the work of art constructs is in some way representative of the larger world which enters into it, which is reflected and portrayed in it; we must firstly therefore use these terms quite carefully. We thus expect the work of art to be something like a projection of a larger reality onto a smaller context, one enclosed and therefore open to view. That is to say, what we cannot get an overview of in the larger world because of its so to speak infinite interlacing, is compressed in the work of art, and reduced to a surveyable small context. If we consider for example *The Magic Mountain* as a portrait of a certain historical situation in the world, that is because it creates a small microcosm which portrays this great macrocosm. From an ontological point of view the question that now arises is, what is the nature of this relationship of representation? What does it mean, in other words, that an infinite world-system, punctuated by numerous unsurveyable accidents, can be represented by a finite, fully enclosed system?

Lukács: Yes—you understand that if I am to answer this, I must again go somewhat further. It is characteristic of the world of human society that those acting within it must have a definite picture of it, in terms of which they act. Now undoubtedly the higher animals also have certain pictures of this kind; they are, I would say, in a position to form mental images. By mental image here I mean a definite and observable phenomenon, directly associated with their life, and which can be extraordinarily precise. Animals recognize this association very exactly; for example any hen, if some bird of prey is hovering over the hen-house, will give the cock a sign and they will both conceal themselves. But the real question is whether the being of the bird of prey is thus comprehended in thought. In my opinion, it is not. In my *Aesthetic* I took the example of the spider, in the centre of whose web one puts a fly. The spider does not recognize in this case that this is the same fly that it always likes to gobble up when it gets caught in its web. For 'fly' is for the spider simply that which gets caught in its web and can then be eaten. Neither the spider, nor even the higher animals, arrive at a concept of the fly. The concept of things only becomes necessary in labour, if concept is to mean something that becomes independent of the occasion of life-preserving perceptions in such a way that, for instance, the bird of prey in a cage is the same bird of prey that swoops through the air. The mental image alone cannot accomplish this identification, and from this arises the whole universe of the world of thought. In the course of human socialization the concept becomes ever more important, in close association with labour. For it is beyond question, I believe, that sciences such as mathematics and geometry, which are today so highly developed, originally arose from labour, and I must put in a word on this subject.

In the labour process, a whole sphere of life, i.e. science, grew up out of what was originally one particular aspect of labour, the deliberation whether a certain stone was or was not suitable for a particular purpose. This development took place quite gradually, and I don't want to go now into all the details of how science was formed. I would just like to say summarily that we men gradually attained in this way a consciousness of the objective character of the world, a consciousness which provides a picture of reality, naturally with the necessary ontological control. Of course the ontological control is itself something historic, insofar as in certain circumstances particular relationships, which objectively are not relationships at all, but only seem to be, appear to be ontologically necessary divisions. I have in mind the example of the ancient idea of the sublunary and superlunary worlds, for the distinction between the great and unequivocal mathematical order of the superlunary world and the chaotic nature of the sublunary world was for the men of antiquity an insuperable ontological obstacle, and forced them to a dualistic conception—we can still see this in Aristotle. When later a more complex and more dynamic cosmology was developed, with Galileo's laws of falling bodies, this dualism vanished completely, and it no longer plays any role in contemporary ontological ideas. I am trying to show with this that ontological criticism of science is not a simple critical activity, which any professor who feels like it can exploit, but a great historic process, in which through labour and through social activity certain modes of representation which are ontologically false are gradually superseded. Thus science acquires a consciousness of reality with an ever stronger tendency to free itself from the historical and ontological foundations which determined its genesis. On the whole this process of dissolution is successful, since in order to understand Pythagoras's theorem, for example, we do not need to know the circumstances in which it was produced, although there certainly was an objective ontological foundation of this kind.

I now come to art. I don't want to get involved now with the very heterogenous origin of the arts, for in my opinion, as you can see from my *Aesthetic*, art did not have a unitary genesis, but gradually attained what I would call an approximate synthesis, so that we can see certain common principles in the various arts. I have also put forward in the *Aesthetic* the idea that conceptual scientific understanding presupposes a dis-anthropomorphizing, by which I mean that we free ourselves as far as possible from the limitations that our sense impressions and our normal thought impose on us. Since we have become familiar with infra-red and ultra-violet rays, for example, since we can identify ultrasonic frequencies and so on, we have already crossed the anthropomorphic limits of our existence. But in society, in which we do all this and everything else, we live a human life. And since we live a human life, we install something which is nowhere present in nature, i.e. the antithesis of the valuable and the not-valuable.

I believe that here again something very simple is involved. Primitive man, whom I already introduced earlier, selected some kind of stone. One stone is suitable to cut a branch, the other not, and this fact—suitable or unsuitable—poses a completely new question, which could not arise in inorganic nature, for if a stone rolls down from a mountain, there is no question of success or failure involved in whether it rolls down in one piece or splinters into two or a hundred pieces. From the standpoint of inorganic nature this is completely immaterial, whilst in the simplest form of labour, the problem of the useful and the non-useful, the suitable and the unsuitable, already involves a concept of value. As labour develops, the ideas of value implicit in it become ever more comprehensive, and the question is posed, ever more intricately and at an ever higher level, whether a particular element in a process which is becoming ever more social and complicated, is or is not suitable for the self-repro-duction of mankind. Here, in my opinion, is the ontological origin of what we call value, and from this antithesis of the valuable and the not valuable a completely new category now arises, which is basically what it is in social life that is meaning-ful or meaningless. Here you are faced with a great historic process. Meaningful life was originally simply identical with social conformity, and it long remained so. Consider for example the famous epitaph of the Spartans who fell at Thermopylae: a meaningful life for them was to obey their laws and die for Sparta. Even in the most heterogenous complexes of social life, a man must act in a unified way, for he must also reproduce his own life. Thus something arose which we call the individual personality of a man. Here also you can see an ontological gradation. Leibniz once showed the princesses of Hanover that there are no two leaves of the same tree that are identical with one another. Leibniz's two leaves turned up again in the nine-teenth century, when it was discovered that there are no two people who have the same fingerprints. But this is only the philo-sophical category of individuality. The development of this individuality into a personality belongs to the realm of social ontology.

I believe, now, that art in its developed form similarly refers back to man himself. It is not for man's sake that objective reality has to be understood as it is independent of man. The reason why I have to try and consider it in its independence is that otherwise I cannot work. If my desires, inclinations etc. are not reflected, not just in the teleological project of labour, but in its execution by means of causal series, I will evidently fail. But there is this other point of view, in which this totality of projects is referred back to man. And this reference back is common to the various different starts made towards art, such as cave painting, primitive dance, and the beginnings of the transition from building to architecture. We should not forget that building is something much earlier than architecture. Here we have a standardized tendency to refer the whole of reality to the development of man, or, as I say in the *Aesthetic*, to the self-consciousness of man. And I would say therefore that art in the ontological sense is a reproduction of the process, how man regards his own life in society and nature, with all problems, all principles etc. that determine his life, positively and negatively, referred back to himself. And so art is not somehow separated from its genesis in a disanthropomorphizing way—which is something of extraordinary importance for ontology. We can understand Homer, to refer once again to a formulation of Marx's, only as the childhood of humanity. If we tried to understand Homer's characters as contemporary men, we would only produce complete nonsense; we rather experience Homer or the other ancient poets as our own past. We can only properly approach the past of humanity through the medium of art; the great facts of history alone only give us a variation of different structures. It is precisely the mission of art to show that within these variations there was a continuity of human behaviour towards society and nature.

Holz: May I throw in at this point a supplementary question? I believe that the concept of a characteristic past which earlier works of art evoke or produce in our minds does not quite meet the purpose, for we certainly also experience in some past works of art, though not in all, something like present-time, as Walter Benjamin once called it. In other words, the content of this past work of art is reactivated by its present significance for us. The theme of Sophocles's *Antigone* could perhaps continually recur in different social situations, as a present problem and not only as one belonging to the childhood of humanity.

Lukács: Look, I would like to go back once again to simple everyday life. Each man has a specific consciousness, a specific memory of his childhood. If you consider your own childhood, you will find certain quite distinct types of experience. There are certain things which appear to you today as purely anecdotal, as it were, which have no connection with your present mental and moral existence. On the other hand you will find that you did and said in your childhood certain things which foreshadow *in nuce* your entire present ego. We must consider the past ontologically and not in the sense of epistemology. If I consider the past epistemologically, then something from the past is simply past. Ontologically however the past is not always simply past, but exerts an influence on the present—not of course the entire past, but parts of it and not always the same parts. I would like to take you back once more to your own development: in your development different aspects of your childhood certainly played different roles at different times. This whole process of conservation in art, which I see as a memory of the past of humanity, is thus a very complicated one. I need only recall that by the end of antiquity Homer was almost forgotten, and until the beginning of the modern era was completely displaced by Virgil; it was in Virgil that the men of the Middle Ages discovered their childhood. Bourgeois culture had to arise—the English critics, for example, who used to play Homer off against Virgil, or Vico in the eighteenth century—in order for humanity to link up with Homer as its own past. A similar development took place with Shakespeare. There is thus a fluctuation in what is considered as living world literature or world art; consider for example how such an important art historian as Burckhardt completely rejected mannerism and baroque, and what a renaissance of mannerism there is today.

It should be evident to anyone that this memory is itself a historic process, and that if I consider memory and the past, I am constrained precisely on that account to conceive these as ontological moments of the living development of humanity, not as an epistemological articulation of time into past, present and future—which can have its meaning in certain special scientific connections. It is not true, however, as Benjamin believed, that something from the past, if it becomes present, springs up out of the past. My greatest childhood experience was when, at nine years old, I read a Hungarian prose translation of the *Iliad*; the fate of Hector, i.e. the fact that the man who suffered a defeat was in the right and was the better hero, was determinant for my entire later development. This is evidently fixed in Homer, and if it were not so fixed, it could not have this effect. However it is equally clear that not everyone read the *Iliad* in this way. Just think of the difference between Dante's conception of Brutus and that of the Renaissance, and you will see the distinction I am making. Here is a great process, a continuous process, from which every epoch extracts that which serves its own ends.

I am here again, if you like, reversing traditional scholarship. Comparative literary history believes that the question is one of influence: *Götz von Berlichingen* influenced the novels of Walter Scott, etc. I believe that in reality things happen completely differently, as I sought to show in my book *The Historical Novel*. As a consequence of the French Revolution, the Napoleonic Wars, etc. literature was confronted with the problem of historicity, which, as you know, did not yet exist for it in the eighteenth century. Insofar as Walter Scott was personally concerned, he found a point of support in *Götz von Berlichingen*, following Molière's saying, *Je prends mon bien où je le trouve*, although *Götz von Berlichingen* was written for quite different reasons. This has the extraordinarily important consequence for the ontology of art, that only those works of art can endure that are connected, in a broad and deep sense, with the development of humanity as humanity, and are therefore susceptible to the most varied forms of interpretation. If you follow up the history of the effects of Homer or Shakespeare or Goethe, you will find that the whole development of consciousness of the later age is reflected there in pro and contra. We now come to the very important problem that there are, on the other hand, works of art or so-called works of art which react in a very lively manner to certain problems of the day, but are unable to develop these to the level of those problems which in some way or another, positively or negatively, play a role in the development of humanity, and which therefore date very rapidly. I can speak here as an old man. There were writers in my youth who won unprecedented acclaim and were taken up quite enthusiastically —I cite such names as Maeterlinck, D'Annunzio, etc.—yet who today have become unreadable. Literary and artistic history also is naturally in part a living process, in part a mass grave.

The specialist disciplines can lead us to a false idea; because such a discipline is in a position to work over all past phenomena, the illusion arises that these things were really in living connection with the continuing memory of human development. This is not simply a question of good and bad. If you take the dramatists of the Elizabethan era, for example, very many of them were important writers. However, if I pass over one or two episodic effects, then Shakespeare has been the only vital force of this era. Now it would be interesting to investigate why Shakespeare has had this effect and not the others. Marlowe, Ford and Webster are certainly alive as far as the teaching of English philology is concerned; but for human development they are not. Here also scientific practice obscures a real connection, instead of explaining it.

To take up the point about Benjamin once again: this element of direct effect on the present is characteristic of any kind of art, and such an effect can occur in a deep or a superficial manner. If it happens in a superficial way, it is simply a passing fashion. If it happens in a deep way, however, the writer in question will be continually resurrected, even if perhaps only at intervals of a hundred years. The eternal ingredient in literature and art really has a much greater stability than we are accustomed to grant it. In classical antiquity this was indicated simply by which manuscripts were preserved and which were not. In our time a similar selection is still in process, and excludes quite relentlessly things which concern merely superficial problems. I recall once again how, as a youth of fifteen or sixteen years, I read the first works of the German naturalists. I fell down in hero-worship at their ability to reproduce the nuances of everyday speech, and saw in this a tremendous artistic advance. Today we can see that this was something quite inconsequential, and if certain works of the young Hauptmann are admired, it is not for their naturalistic dialogue, but on quite other grounds. And in just the same way today, as a result of an extraordinarily strong manipulation, the discovery of a new technique of expression is considered something of intrinsic value. If you take the present-day German critics, they will generally consider an interior monologue favourably, while someone who produces something without interior monologue is immediately considered old-fashioned. The presence or absence of interior monologue, however, is a question of form quite secondary to the content. Semprun's *The Long Voyage*, for example, is written entirely in interior monologue, and in my opinion it is one of the most important products of socialist realism—you must excuse me for using this expression, I am a conservative—and so interior monologue and socialist realism are in no way mutually exclusive.

Holz: We have now reached a point at which we can perhaps clarify a very prevalent misunderstanding about your concept of realism. Normally your distinction between realist and nonrealist art is understood in such a way that the realist work would simply have absorbed more actuality than the non-realist. If, however, I take up the statement you have just made, that the only works of art which can endure are those which stand in a broad and deep connection with the development of humanity, then that does not exclude other works of art having also absorbed a very dense reality, but one which precisely does not have a future perspective, a deep perspective for the development of humanity. In other words, realism and non-realism in the work of art do not refer to the contemporary reality that is reflected, but to the historical perspective and indeed precisely to the future perspective which it should put forward.

Lukács: Yes, this is a question on which I am in fundamental opposition to literary and artistic history. The matter is very simple. I take a somewhat caricatured example. It can be said for example that *Götz von Berlichingen* is a realist work, while *Iphigenie* is non-realist, since it is written in verse. Such ideas are of course put forward, and there are certainly cases in which realism and non-realism coincide with antitheses such as these; one can perhaps see this in such important individuals as Schiller and Richard Wagner, who as a result of certain idealistic notions and theatrical customs, transgressed the realism of their own intentions. Think for example how in *Maria Stuart* Schiller completely distorts Queen Elizabeth in order to satisfy his moral principles. On the other hand—and this is now the real contradiction which I am speaking of—I regard the opposition of naturalism and realism as one of the greatest oppositions in aesthetics. In my aesthetic writings you will constantly come across this opposition, while even such important art historians as those of the Riegl school treat naturalism and realism as almost synonymous. This is absolutely incorrect. For example, the forerunners and creators of German impressionism used an unprecedented number of naturalist elements, while in impressionism proper and what arose from it—Manet and the young Monet, Sisley and Pisarro, and particularly Cézanne—the naturalistic tendency is as good as completely absent. Art history ignores a very essential problem if it conceives realism and naturalism as one and the same. I will not go into details here, since you are familiar with my writings and know quite well how much these questions have occupied me, and how for example in my little pamphlet on modern art I criticized the socialist realism of the Stalin era by calling it an establishment naturalism. What was advertised as 'socialist realism', and is today used to compromise this term, is in my opinion not only not socialist realism, but not realism at all, simply an establishment naturalism.

If we are speaking of the concept of realism, what I mean by this is a kind of literature which, in polemical writings about the Soviet era, I called realism from Homer to Gorky. I took this in a literal sense, without wishing to compare Gorky with Homer, rather in order to say that a common tendency is involved, which is not one of techniques of expression, of style, etc., but rather an orientation to the real, essential nature of mankind, persisting through a developmental process. The problem of realism is related to this, and so realism is naturally not a stylistic concept. Rather, the art of any time—and this is the essential thing—relates the immediate problems of its age to the general development of mankind and links them with it, a connection which may of course be quite hidden from the writer himself. I certainly do not mean that Homer had a certain idea of mankind, and it is because of this that, in the scene in which old Priam travels to Achilles to return the corpse of Hector, he raises a great human problem which, in a certain sense, no one can ignore today if, as I would say, he wants to settle accounts with the past and with himself. That is what I have in mind when I speak of the memory of humanity. Here, incidentally, there is a connection with Hegelian philosophy, for you will remember that the concluding section of the *Phenomenology of Mind*, in which Hegel discusses absolute mind, is presented as a 're-collection', as opposed to 'externalization'.

In Hegel, however, the moment of the past thereby becomes far too dominating, while in my conception the past is on the one hand past, one's own experience, but on the other hand it contributes a theme towards taking up a position in the present. And this theme has been taken up by every society up till now which has returned to certain definite moments of the past. Think of the French Revolution's preoccupation with classical antiquity. It is quite irrelevant in practice whether Robespierre or Saint-Just had a correct conception of the ancient world. The point is that Robespierre and Saint-Just could not have behaved the way they did if they had not given antiquity this place in their own thinking, thus in the motivation behind their teleological projects. In this way the memory of humanity locks art into its own past, and I would like to say that at certain moments an individual human life acquires such a significance that it becomes similar to a work of art. The life of Socrates would be an example of this, and from this standpoint it is completely immaterial whether Jesus actually existed or not, whether or not his character is correctly portrayed in the gospels. There is an image of Jesus which has been an animating force from the crisis of the dissolving slave economy until today—think only of Dostoyevsky's Grand Inquisitor—and which one must deal with in one way or another. And it is not only a matter of Dostoyevsky—the paradigm also has its effects on science, if you consider for example Max Weber's *Politics as a Vocation*, where he contrasts *Realpolitik* and the Sermon on the Mount, and attempts to extract from the latter an approach to political behaviour. This shows that, quite independent of historical accuracy, the character of Jesus has acquired a similar significance for humanity as the character of Antigone or Hamlet or Don Quixote. I would say, in passing, that such figures may well influence a very great proportion of our behavioural options. The character of Napoleon, for example, exerted a tremendous influence in the nineteenth century, from Rastignac to Raskolnikov, although there was no single literary work in which Napoleon himself was adequately portrayed. This precisely demonstrates an ever increasing ontological requirement, which in its essentials is satisfied by art. What I have said today about Jesus does not contradict this, it only shows that those tendencies which lead from the development of art to the construction of myth, create in this case also a similar quite specific requirement for art. We see for example in Homer, what role the exemplary character of earlier heroes plays in the deeds of his own. Art and its contents touch on the essentials of human development, using the technical forms existing at the time, but in its ultimate effect it is independent of this technique, and this is how art has its long-term effect.

Holz: When you speak of the realist aspects of works of art, are you always referring to this capacity, to these preformed aspects of content . . .

Lukács: Yes.

Holz: Is it not the case then, that there is also a kind of realism which is distinguished by opening up to humanity certain formal devices. I am thinking for example of literature, since it has to do with language; is not the conquest of new linguistic possibilities and the preparation of new linguistic modes for human usage also something which must be included in the concept of realism? I would certainly say that Cervantes is a realist, but is not Góngora also a realist, in his elaboration of certain linguistic figures and possibilities which can then be passed down to future generations as forms of expression of linguistic thought?

Lukács: This cannot be regarded as a purely formal problem. I believe it is one of the greatest misfortunes of our times that the whole of art is considered from the standpoint of technical formalism. Just as there is a discussion in fashion about the miniskirt, so there is now a discussion about op art and pop art and so on, which takes place almost at the level of a fashion show. This conception is given theoretical form by those so-called schools of interpretation which blow up purely formal problems of linguistic innovation into major problems in their own right. I come back once again to basic ontology: language is a means of communication between people, not simply a piece of information; if I say to a woman, 'I love you', that is not a piece of information, but something quite different. And if Herr Professor Bense makes up a theory and discusses whether declarations of love have a coefficient of 448 or 487, that has nothing to do with the question of declarations of love. Do you understand what I mean by that? Now the question again arises: if this linguistic innovation contributes something essential to a correct and deepened conception of the world, then it will pass into ordinary usage, and then the matter has, I would say, lost its innovatory component. Otherwise it remains something purely external. Thus for example is was an unquestionable linguistic innovation for the German naturalists at the end of the nineteenth century to reproduce in their dialogue the Silesian, Swabian and Berlin accents. This played a definite role as a way of superseding the Wildenbruch-type uniformity of dramatic speech, but after a certain time it as good as completely vanished, and in the place of dialect other ways of individualizing speech were developed without this naturalism, such as you can find for example in the dialogue of Thomas Mann and others. Thus I am of the opinion that in this case the content is in a decisive sense primary. We should not base ourselves on technical premises, but should rather ask what great value of an era a certain technique of language, painting, etc. implies and brings forward, and what part of it then passes over into future development. I naturally consider it an interesting problem of technical construction, what a contemporary writer can do with the language of Góngora; in my opinion it is indeed very interesting that certain technical discoveries are made which later become, in the hands of people stimulated by them, something quite different from the original intention. Take for example the linguistic discoveries of surrealism. There is no question but that they had a great influence on the lyrics of Eluard. But there is also no question that Eluard's really great poems are something more than surrealistic language. In these, surrealistic language has become an element of a complex whole which expresses something essential for contemporary subjectivity.

Second Conversation

Georg Lukács—Leo Kofler

Society and the Individual

Kofler: Herr Lukács, it impressed me enormously yesterday how you took simple things and brought them to bear on extraordinarily complicated problems. I would like to use a similar method today and again begin with some more simple problems . . .

Lukács: Very good . . .

Kofler: . . . as a way of advancing onto the complicated ones. One quite specific question has both interested and occupied me for a long time already. It has become customary for bourgeois ideology tendentiously to equate ideology with false consciousness and to similarly equate its own free-floating consciousness —supposedly free-floating—with unconstrained consciousness. In this way it can draw certain ideological conclusions. The following problem thus arises: the working class, which still today forms half the population, is triumphantly informed that it has become bourgeois. What is meant by this is that the worker formerly had a false class consciousness, but today has a correct one, insofar as he has accepted a bourgeois consciousness. This involves a contradiction, as the working class is ascribed a constrained class consciousness which is nevertheless correct, while correct consciousness is simultaneously equated by definition with unconstrained consciousness. Is this contradiction essential to bourgeois ideology, or is it merely contingent?

Lukács: You must allow me once again to simplify the question somewhat. I believe that Gramsci was quite right in drawing attention to the fact that we generally use the word ideology in two quite different senses. On the one hand it refers to the elementary Marxist axiom that every person in society has a

41

definite class position, one aspect of which, of course, is the over-all culture of his time, and that there can thus be no item of consciousness which is not determined by the here and now of the existing situation. On the other hand this leads to certain definite deformations, and we have now come to understand ideology also in the sense of a certain deformed reaction to reality. I believe that in using the concept of ideology we must keep these two things separate, and in order to do this we must start from the fact that man is first and foremost, like every organism, a being that responds to his environment—which brings me back to the ontological question. In other words, man reconstructs the problems arising from his real existence as questions, and then responds to them; there is no such thing at all as a free-floating consciousness, existing on its own basis, and working purely from the inside outwards, and no one has managed to demon-strate such a thing. I believe that the so-called free-floating in-telligentsia, just as the slogan, so beloved today, of the end of ideology, is a pure fiction, with no relation to the real condition of real people in real human society.

Kofler: The question is occasionally raised in this connection whether there do not exist ideological phenomena indifferent to class, i.e. phenomena in the superstructure which are not deter-mined by class position. You yourself, Herr Professor Lukács, have already stressed very sharply in earlier works that ideology does not simply involve a direct class tie, but is rather an aspect of the totality of class society. However one can still discover certain ideological phenomena which are factually class-indifferent in the sense that they are associated equally with the bourgeoisie, the proletariat and the petty bourgeoisie—these phenomena occur for example in the sphere of language, and above all in the terminology characteristic of the world of reification. For ex-ample: 'We are dominated by technology', 'The atom bomb threatens us', 'Inflation makes everything dearer', or 'Massifica-tion derives from mass society'—Marx once said ironically that 'Want is here derived from *pauverté*'. Nevertheless these reified forms of speech can not be classified merely by their association with a *specific* class; they are rather class-indifferent, although certainly not independent of class society, for they are indeed mirror images of a definite mode of behaviour in a reified and fetishized social situation.

Lukács: I would here again go somewhat further. Since human life is based on a metabolism with nature, it goes without saying that certain truths which we acquire in the process of carrying out this metabolism have a general validity—for example the truths of mathematics, geometry, physics and so on. However, the bourgeoisie have made a fetish out of this, for these truths can in certain circumstances be very closely linked with class struggles. If we say today that the truths of astronomy are not class-bound, that is certainly correct; however, when the theories of Copernicus and Galileo were under discussion, to take up a position for or against Galileo was one of the most important determinants of class standpoint. Since the metabolism between human society and nature is also a social process, it is always possible for concepts obtained from it to react on the class struggles in a society. If I now consider such concepts as development, progress, etc., these are less precise terms. In and for itself development is a fact which we can speak about independently of class—as, for example, the Darwinian concept of the development of species. On the other hand, the very question of Darwinism was for decades a social issue. Whether humanity has a unitary development, or whether civilization begins and ends in different centres in a cyclical movement, is similarly not a question that can be answered irrespective of the class divisions of a society.

I believe that there are movable limits involved here, for on the one hand human understanding is in a position to establish certain things that are valid for the whole of human society, possibly even for the entire natural order, irrespective of how they are valued by different classes, while on the other hand every man is involved in social struggles with his whole personality, so that acceptance or denial of any one statement is potentially class-determined. I therefore believe that we cannot

iversal division: here ideology ends and something
ns. The division is movable, in a state of flux; it is
y the social structure of the time and the state of
the   uggles related to this, and is not founded in the
abstract statement itself. Exactly the same holds for the so-called
free-floating classes. In quiet periods, for example, when things
do not come to a head, there are unquestionably situations in
which a class can take a quite neutral position towards even
the dominant social struggles. However, I believe I can say quite
categorically that one can never say in advance of any human
individual that he will behave indifferently in all possible class
conflicts. Indifference is certainly possible, as well as the most
improbable connections, and this is exactly what gives history
its motley complexion. You will remember how in England, in
the first half of the nineteenth century, the conservative aristocracy went against the bourgeoisie and made possible certain
reforms of labour conditions, in particular a reduction in working
hours. Now to draw from this the conclusion that the aristocracy
had a class interest in the reduction of working hours would be
too far-reaching, although this is not simply a contingent fact,
but an understandable action of this class, corresponding to the
class struggles of that time. In my opinion, we have to uphold
the dialectical axiom that the truth is concrete, even in the case
of ideology.

Kofler: I believe we are dealing here with an extraordinarily
important elucidation. I would like now to concentrate on one
particular point, for the simple reason that it is discussed frequently in our own milieu. You have spoken of the flux, the
transition and the persistence of concepts, of a generaliza-
tion . . .

Lukács: Yes . . .

Kofler: . . . with respect to the concept of progress, for example,
I would perhaps call these concepts of abstraction. Now the
question as to how this abstraction takes place arises again and
again, and here one comes up against the problem of irrationalism. There is no doubt of the existence of irrationalism as an

44

orientation of the human psyche. I am referring to intuition, to the free-floating idea, to the creative power, if you put it that way. Now you have time and again in your writings attacked the problem of irrationalism, and have also indicated its dangers in the area of concept formation, of ideological concrctization. What is meant by this is perhaps that the internal flux of life becomes independent and is overemphasized as against rationality, so that experience, internal experience, is made out to be the real world—we are already dealing here with very modern problems. Then there is the question of mythologizing, of opposing *internal* truth to *ratio* and reason. Related to this and in the same irrational manner, the concept of progress is also denied. The logical conclusion of all this is that humanism is mocked as not in conformity with experience, with the 'really valuable', with the 'special nature of the inner man'. Thus humanism prevails externally, but the other attitude in a subtle way prevails internally. It would interest me to know how you would expand on or interpret this question, independently now of the problem of irrationalism in German history, to which I will return later.

Lukács: Yes—you see, I would first of all like to dispense with the extraordinarily popular theme of the opposition between intuition and intellect. Considered epistemologically, this is totally false and has no basis whatsoever. As a purely psychological concept intuition speaks for itself, and takes place constantly. As against the mythologization of this concept we should emphasize the fact that intuition always occurs when a man is yery occupied with some kind of complex of thoughts, and when, after this complex has been at work subconsciously in his mind for a while, suddenly—I say 'suddenly' in quotation marks—he comes to a result. Such intuition you will find right through to mathematics, it has no particularly close connection with art. However—and now comes the epistemological side— it says nothing for or against any statement that it was produced intuitively or not. A statement must be proved, either logically or historically, and its truth must be checked quite independently of how it was produced. I regard this as an important stipulation, for in German philosophy since Schelling, and in a certain sense already in Kant's *Critique of Judgement*, intuitive knowledge has been ascribed a certain superiority over non-intuitive knowledge, without in my opinion any epistemological reason ever being introduced or even attempted. The superiority of intuition was accepted as a kind of dogma. This is the subjective side, as it were.

As for the objective side, I believe that in real human praxis the idea of *ratio* has been used for thousands of years in a sense very much opposed to *ratio* in a real and reasonable sense. I believe that that is rational which agrees with our experience in labour and our mastery of reality, i.e. when I find a relationship which actually functions. If I let a stone fall from my hand and it drops to the ground, and if I repeat this experiment a few times, then we have a reasonable relationship, which Galileo formulated at a high level in his laws of falling bodies. Every real rationality which we find in life is an 'if-then' rationality. Any kind of concrete situation is linked with concrete implications and because it recurs in our life in a lawful way, we correctly call such a relationship rational. However an exaggerated sense of logic, of what is attainable through logic, has endowed the world with a universal rationality which in fact does not exist. I believe that it is rational, according to the laws of nature that prevail today, for a stone to drop down to the ground. But if I imagine another world in which the stone flew upward and would regularly fly upward, then the people of such a world would conceive that as equally rational, so that it is not for some kind of rational reason that the stone drops, but rather that this is prescribed for it because nature is just so. That is what this 'if-then' rationality means.

Now in human society, in social development, situations constantly arise in which what yesterday appeared rational suddenly no longer agrees with the facts, and we are faced with the equivalent in the social sphere of the upward-flying stone. In this case human beings can take up two types of position. One position is that which man regularly takes up towards nature in labour: if a material object shows itself to be, so to speak, refractory in terms of the former laws, then you experiment on it, using other interpretations, until the new lawfulness has been discovered. This process also happens continually in social development. On the other hand for certain classes—and here we return once more to the class question—this change in social reality is completely meaningless, and they find in it nothing other than anarchy and disorder, in the social sense. You need only consider the position of the different classes in the French Revolution: things that seemed very simple and rational to the revolutionary classes were nevertheless viewed by the former ruling classes and those who sympathized with them as chaotic and irrational. Since our thoughts always depend on our social position and stand in relationship to it, situations continually arise in history in which major social classes and major thinkers representing them react, in certain cases, by considering and condemning the new social relationships and the new development of society from the standpoint of the old *ratio*. You should not forget that if, in the French Revolution, supporters of the feudal class of that time frequently took up an irrational standpoint, in the time of Thomas Aquinas feudalism was in no way irrational. Thomas Aquinas was correct to conceive feudalism as something simply following from reason, for very much in the social reality of his time corresponded to 'if-then' rationality. However the praxis of Marat and Robespierre could not be fitted into the rational system of the feudal classes, and so what we call irrationalism arose out of the social situation.

It is characteristic of modern development that the new *ratio* was not simply questioned and denied, but a specific system of irrationalism was constructed, which then spread extraordinarily far afield and showed its implications in things that—as I would say—the original initiators of this system did not desire at all. I will give two examples to illustrate this. Consider the political sociology of Max Weber, in particular his doctrine in 'Politics as a Vocation' to the effect that the world is governed by different gods. What lies behind this is that Max Weber, in the

society he was faced with, could not possibly arrive at an unambiguous concept of 'if-then' *ratio*, but remained fixated to the
struggle of these different ethical principles which he did not
want to reduce further. Such a reduction would have led to consequences that he could not integrate, and so he took refuge, so
to speak, in the mythological conception of gods struggling
against one another. One could say . . . I believe one can safely
say, that at this point irrationalism also invades Max Weber's
system.

Take on the other hand a system of ideas such as neo-
positivism, which restricts the whole world to a manipulated
rationality and rejects everything that would transgress this
limit. Now originally neo-positivism had a real thinker as one
of its founders, namely Wittgenstein. And Wittgenstein, who
founded the neo-positivist positions really philosophically, saw
quite clearly that on the margin of these positions, if I might put
it this way, there lay a desert of irrationalism, about which
nothing rational could be said from the neo-positivist standpoint.
Wittgenstein, however, was much too intelligent to believe that
the world beyond the statements of positivism did not exist, and
on the margin of Wittgenstein's philosophy there is, I believe, a
terrain of irrationality—this is not simply my own observation,
but one that many others have made. And so I believe we have
experienced, in the course of the nineteenth and twentieth
centuries, a great wave of irrationalism, in the most varied forms.
You are quite right that this is not confined to Germany; American pragmatism, for example, has irrationalist aspects, Bergson is
a quite typical example of irrationalism, Croce, whatever his own
opinion, is full of irrationalist elements. No one will deny all
this, and so irrationalism is in no way a purely German phenomenon, but an international one. All that is specific to Germany
is that irrationalism there became the ideology of a reactionary
political power, indeed the most reactionary power, which in
other countries was not the case.

Kofler: You occasionally define this German irrationalism as a
belief in internal invincibility—in internal powers which stand

opposed to the external rational ones. Doesn't this exaggerated belief in an internal mental process which is allegedly opposed to the external social world have to be related to German history— as you have to a certain extent done, perhaps even to the entire unfortunate history of Germany? We could begin with the defeat of the Knights of the Teutonic Order in 1410 and 1466, then there is the partition of the Order's Baltic states in 1561, the displacement of trade routes, the Thirty Years War with all its consequences, the whole really unfortunate history of the defeat of the peasants—you have certainly mentioned all these points, even if in scattered places. Now, what often interests students in seminars is your demonstration that in Germany there is a prevailing tendency to seek irrational solutions, by stylizing the unresolved problems to be answered; how can this be concretely explained, and why precisely in Germany did irrationalist ideology win total domination in a specific and exaggerated form, and become an essential characteristic of the German nation—in a historic sense, of course?

Lukács: I believe that it really is related to specific aspects of German history, and certainly to the fact that certain forms of philosophy and social science, which we can group together for the moment under the term *ratio*, were produced in the great nations of the West by people of those countries themselves. I believe that the coalescence of the nation into a political unit is closely related to the rise of modern society. It is natural for any Frenchman or Englishman to perceive this as his own act, without undue consideration. I believe it was the French ratio that, from the concentrating influence of absolutism through to the French Revolution and beyond, combined the French people into a unity; independent action, being a man and a patriot, coincided completely. German development, on the contrary, was marked by the inability of the German people to combine themselves into a nation, into a modern nation, and so a kind of schism arose in the internal emotional life of the authentic German, who found himself still involved in the old reality. If his reason led him to understand that the old reality had become impossible, he still could not find any politically viable solution. There was thus a contradiction, which emerged in Germany in the eighteenth century with Justus Möser, Herder, and the young Goethe. Domestic revolution would possibly have been able to alter things, but the external and internal conditions for this were absent in Germany, and it is again no accident that such a great opponent of irrationalism as Hegel saw in Napoleon on the one hand the *Weltgeist* on horseback, on the other hand the great constitutionalist in Paris who was in a position to put German affairs into some kind of order.

This dualism persisted up to the fiasco of the 1848 revolution, and essentially the so-called revolution from above was a complicated solution, since the irrational appearance of an externality that was internalized, and an internality which was really external, became so contorted that the German people's own powers were of no avail. This is the basis of all those dualisms which were later filled out under the influence of various theories, partly coming from abroad, to the effect that there is an original human substance standing in hostile relation to the progressive development of the external world. That was not simply Hitler's doctrine; it is already complete in Klage's thesis of the mind as adversary of the soul, and it is similarly a basic axiom of Heidegger's ideology, with the notion of 'thrown-ness'. Hitler simply made a palpable demagogy out of it, by making the bearer of this internality the ancient, racially pure German. As a result of Germany's delay in becoming a nation, and doing so not from its own internal forces, a special social situation came about which contrasts not only with the Western countries, but also, and extremely sharply, with Russian development. In Russia the social structure was indeed more backward, but national unity had already been created by absolutism, and there was therefore, from the French Revolution onwards, via the Decembrists and right up till 1917, an irrepressible train of insurrections against tsarism. There was no comparable movement in Germany. I therefore stress again and again that there is here a past which the Germans have not yet mastered, and that they could not deal with Hitler because they had not yet dealt with their entire past, because the Germans still do not have the self-consciousness of a self-created and progressive history.

The only things that Germany created for itself were reactionary—Bismarck's empire, Hitler's reich and so on can in a certain sense be regarded as self-created—and it is no accident that during the entire twentieth century liberalism and democracy have been regarded in Germany as imported goods which is still the case today to a large extent. It is not true that only socialism is regarded in this way. You can find a great number of theorists who also reject liberalism and democracy as Western importations which do not agree with the real German nature. They identify this real German nature with the compromise that arose in the Bismarckian form of the German empire, simply from the irresistible requirements of economic development—something which the historians absolutely refuse to recognize. I believe that out of every ten books that are written about Bismarck, you will only find *one* in which it is at least maintained that the empire Bismarck created was, at bottom, the Prussian Zollverein. What Bismarck united into a state was not the German people but the Prussian Zollverein. I regard this as very important, but one could almost say that German historiography completely ignores it. It is significant that Treitschke still recognized this fact, while in the work of later historians such as Marcks, Meinecke, etc. it is as good as completely absent. And hence the whole of German history came into such a chaotic condition that essentially the only solution that was conceived as conforming to German nature was what I would call a reactionary and irrational solution. This is a peculiarity of German irrationalism, which is not so highly developed even in Italian fascism.

Kofler: Herr Lukács, I would like to make use of the rare opportunity we have of being in Budapest to raise a further question in connection with the problem of irrationalism. This is one which is certainly discussed by intellectuals, which also affects the entire Western world, but which does not involve problems of sociology, philosophy, science or literature, but rather the *spontaneous* irrationalism of the masses in the highly industrialized societies. This is an irrationalism of a special kind, which important figures of semi-Marxist or left bourgeois tendency are very concerned about, an irrationalism which is very hard to pin down, and perhaps for this reason is still an unknown quantity; and because it is a quite recent phenomenon of Western society, it is scarcely discussed in your writings. I have promised my students to ask you without fail to take a position on this, and I would like to offer a few specific formulations, so as to make clear precisely what I am talking about.

We are dealing here again with concepts and notions that are almost class-indifferent, if certainly not aloof from the class society that permeates them. 'Voluntary integration', for example, no longer means for the naïve, spontaneous consciousness, as it did originally, 'participation on the basis of rational considerations and decisions', but rather 'participation on the basis of irrationally induced blind consent'. 'Contentment' today no longer means so much rational acceptance of one's lot, or self-satisfaction with a visible result, but implies a manipulated notion directed by the themes of consumer technology, which for its part is again based on manipulation. What makes it evidently clear that we are dealing here with completely irrational processes is that at the same time this ideologically manipulated consumer demand is restricted to a level of ascetic renunciation so as to install an approximate balance between the forced consumption consciousness and the practical material possibilities available to it. Another concept of extraordinary importance in studying the irrational world view of the masses today is the concept of 'privacy'. 'Private' is no longer something opposed to 'public', as it was at one time, but denotes an individual living space which, with ideological assistance, is totally taken over by the influences of the external world, indeed with the individual's own collaboration. Or we could take the concept of 'opposition'. 'Opposition' no longer means refusal to participate, but on the contrary the demand to participate in existing practices—I am thinking here of the SPD. This is approximately what is understood by 'opposition'. 'Freedom', for example, no longer means the right to do, say or wish the opposite to that which all or most do, say or wish, but the right to decide to do what has already been declared to be free in the repressive order. In the repressive order! One could continue these examples indefinitely, but I have not come to Budapest to make speeches, but to request you to take up a position on these matters, in as much detail as you possibly can. I believe this particular problem is of the greatest importance, as it has received hardly any consideration in traditional Marxism, besides a few utterances and, if I may be so immodest, a new book of my own which will be published shortly.

Lukács: That is quite correct, and in my opinion it is related to the economic fact that after the great crisis of 1929 capitalism changed in certain fundamental respects. Not in the sense that it ceased to be capitalism, or that some kind of people's capitalism arose, but in what I believe to be a quite simple sense, which I would like to briefly explain. If you go back eighty or a hundred years, to Marx's time, it was then essentially just the industries producing the means of production that were organized on large-scale capitalist lines. If you add cotton cloth, milling and the sugar industry, you have the basic branches of the capitalist economy, in the strict sense. In the following eighty years the whole of consumption became capitalized. I am not just referring to shoes, confectionery, etc. What is very important is that the household also began to be an object of heavy industry, with all these refrigerators, washing machines, etc., and side by side with this the so-called service sector similarly became part of large-scale capitalism. The semi-feudal domestic servant of Marx's day is becoming ever more of an anachronism, and a capitalist system of services is developing. I first want to deal with a superficial aspect of the matter. Consider a great factory-owner or manufacturer of Marx's time. It is clear that the clientele of such a person was extraordinarily limited; he could dispose of his products without a special large apparatus. However, when an item of mass consumption is produced with the resources of a major industry—just think of something like razor-blades—then a special apparatus is necessary to bring the millions of razor-blades to the individual consumers. I am convinced that the whole system of manipulation which we have spoken of arose on the basis of this economic requirement and that it subsequently extended into society and politics. This apparatus now dominates all external social life, from presidential elections to the consumption of ties and cigarettes, and you only have to turn the pages of any magazine to find sufficient examples of this.

This has another and more far-reaching consequence, insofar as the exploitation of the working class is shifting ever further away from exploitation through absolute surplus value towards exploitation through relative surplus value, which means that a rise in exploitation can even be combined with an increase in the standard of living of the workers. At the time Marx was writing, this kind of thing was only in its earliest stages, though I would not say that it was entirely absent. Marx was, I believe, the first to recognize the economic category of relative surplus value, and Marx said very interestingly, in an unpublished section of *Capital*, that absolute surplus value only subsumes production to capital in a formal sense, and that production is only really subsumed by capitalist relations with the development of relative surplus value, which is precisely the hallmark of our own era. All the problems which you have just spoken of emerge in this connection. The whole problem of alienation acquires a completely new physiognomy. At the time that Marx wrote the *Economic and Philosophic Manuscripts*, the alienation of the working class directly involved a labour that drove the workers down to an almost animal level; alienation was in a certain sense identical with de-humanization, and consequently the class struggle was oriented for decades towards securing a human life for the workers by means of appropriate demands regarding wages and working hours. The celebrated 'three eights' of the Second International were symptomatic of this class struggle.

Today this problem has in a certain sense been displaced, only in a certain sense, of course.

You will remember that when Herr Erhard made his first attempts at economic reform, his first step towards this was to demand a one-hour increase in the working week, a measure which clearly involves absolute surplus value. If you take Wilson's policy in England, you have the same story; absolute surplus value is not dead, it simply no longer plays the dominant role which it did when Marx wrote the *Economic and Philosophic Manuscripts*. What follows from this, then? It follows that a new problem is visible on the working-class horizon, that is the problem of a meaningful life. The class struggle in the era of absolute surplus value was directed towards creating the objective conditions for a meaningful life. Today, with a five-day week and a wage corresponding to this, the first conditions for a meaningful life can already emerge, and as a result the problem has arisen that the manipulation which extends from the purchase of cigarettes through to presidential elections divides human beings from meaningful life by a mental barrier. For manipulation is not, as the official doctrine has it, the desire to inform the consumer what the best refrigerator or the best razor-blade is, but a question of the control of consciousness.

I will just take a single example, the 'Gauloises type'. When someone is to be portrayed as a splendid, active man, this quality is revealed by his smoking Gauloises. Then you can see in an advertisement, I don't know whether it is for soap or for some kind of cream, a young man besieged by two beautiful women, because women find the smell of this soap erotically attractive. I am sure you understand what I mean by this. As a result of this manipulation, the worker, the working person, is forcibly distracted from considering how he could transform his free time into genuine leisure, and it is insinuated that consumption is his own life-fulfilling purpose, exactly as, in the era of the twelve-hour working day, labour itself dominated life in a dictatorially intrusive way.

The complicated problem now is the need to organize a new

form of resistance. If we consider not vulgar Marxism, but genuine Marxism, such as Marx understood it, then it is quite clear that it provides the themes for combating these new forms of alienation. I have in mind the famous passage in the third volume of *Capital*, where Marx writes of the realm of freedom and the realm of necessity. Marx's statement that labour is inevitably always a realm of necessity is very important, but he adds to this that socialist development consists in giving labour forms worthy of human beings and appropriate to human development. You can add to this Marx's remark in the *Critique of the Gotha Programme*, where he lays down as a condition for communism that labour must itself become life's prime want. Now there is today such a thing as scientific management and a way of dealing psychologically with the workers, but this is simply directed towards making the present capitalist technology acceptable to the workers by manipulative means. It is not directed towards creating a technology which could make labour a valued occupation for the workers. A firmly fixed prejudice of ours that I have already mentioned holds that, since capitalism is as it is, since every technological innovation is directed towards increasing profit, and everything else is a side-effect, it is therefore part of the ontological nature of technological developments to stand unconditionally in the service of capitalism.

I will simply adduce one historical example here, a very interesting transition which took place in the late Middle Ages with the beginnings of capitalism. At this time handicrafts were beginning to be perfected in an artistic way. I am not speaking now of high art, but of furniture, tables, chairs etc. as they were made at this time. Capitalism completely wiped away this development, for capitalism precisely introduced different teleological principles to govern technological performance in such things as the construction of a table. Now, just as a handicraftsman of the fifteenth century certainly experienced the rising demands of capitalism as something completely unnatural, so will a present-day technologist see it as completely unnatural and absurd that a plan of production should be directed by the consideration of making production meaningful for the workers, although this kind of technological project is no more new today than today's quantifying mass technology was in its time for the qualitative and artistic technology of the Renaissance. It is easy to forget how far technology is socially conditioned and to make the technological projects of capitalism into some kind of intrinsic feature of human existence. That is the labour side of the matter.

The other side is the transformation of free time into leisure, which can only be achieved by ideological work, by an ideological enlightenment which explains ever more fully how contemporary manipulation runs contrary to the true interests of humanity. Excuse me if I once more take a frivolous example from fashion—I must confess that I always follow the fashion reports with great sociological interest. For the last twenty years haute couture, in its manipulation of women's clothing, has been waging a constant struggle to introduce long skirts at all costs. It is obvious that the profits of the textile industry would be so much the greater—that is quite clear. Fashion, which is said to be all-powerful, fails at this point. For the last twenty years longer skirt lengths have always been predicted before the great Paris fashion shows, but on this point women have defended their rights, for they are not prepared to sit in an over-crowded tram on the way to work in a long skirt. You understand what I mean by this example: manipulation is basically not all-powerful. It is naturally much harder to arouse in people the other, real needs of personal development, and I believe that we are faced here with a very long and laborious process; but it is one which can be victorious in the end just the same.

Indeed, this is no longer something that concerns only the working class; in this respect, as far as relative surplus value is concerned, the entire intelligentsia and the entire bourgeoisie is really just as much subjected to capitalism, and thus to this capitalist manipulation, as the working class. What is at issue here, therefore, is to arouse the genuine independent personality, the possibility of which has been brought about by previous social development. For there is no doubt that the amount of labour necessary for physical human reproduction must constantly fall, and hence the space can develop for a civilized human existence for everyone. In earlier civilizations this only happened in what Marx once called an economically restricted way; slavery in Athens, for example, freed an upper stratum from labour and thus enabled the splendid Athenian culture to arise. It is undeniable that there are strata whose mode of life is still governed by the old categories of capitalism, and it is naturally a major task to show how these categories are disappearing and to demand for the workers concerned a different standard of living. There is, however, no question but that, for a large stratum of working people, both mental and manual workers, conditions are beginning to arise in which, on the basis of the reduction of the labour necessary for reproduction, they are in a position to lead a free life corresponding to their human needs. What we need, therefore, is a major, fundamental portrayal of alienation at its present-day level.

I greatly welcome it that people today are beginning to study the young Marx in this connection. It is really stupid from a historical point of view to play off the young Marx against the mature Marx. The *Economic and Philosophic Manuscripts* show us the phenomenon of alienation in a very formative and philosophical manner. But the pressing problem of alienation today has a different physiognomy from that in Marx's time, a hundred and twenty years ago, and the task is to explain this new form of alienation. The whole historical dialectic of this complex of problems must be brought to bear on this, for there are today extraordinarily clever, bold and good people, for whom I have the greatest human and intellectual esteem, who fall into fetishism and see technical development as a Moloch devouring everything in an irresistible way. This is once again false, and can be shown to be so on the basis of Marxism. Forty years ago I polemicized against Bukharin's concept of technology as the decisive productive force; today this error is even more strongly perpetrated in connection with such great new discoveries as the use of atomic energy.

Our task, the Marxist task, should be to free people's minds from this fetishistic fatalism, to show that technology has always been only a means in the development of the productive forces, that the productive forces are always in the last analysis men and their capacities, and that to take the reform of man as its central task would signify a new stage of Marxism. I believe that there is nothing anti-Marxist about this, for you must not forget that the young Marx even said in his *Critique of Hegel's Philosophy of Right* that the root of things, for man, is man himself. This side of Marxism must now be brought to the fore, not in an empty propagandistic way, but founded on the analysis of contemporary capitalism, and it is in this way that the basis for struggle against contemporary capitalism can be found. That is how, in broad lines, I would reply to your question.

Kofler: Our discussion has certainly established that manipulation is not all-powerful. But this kind of enlightenment has become extraordinarily difficult to carry out. Perhaps I might take your concept of religious atheism out of the context of its association with purely intellectual modes of thought . . .

Lukács: Yes . . .

Kofler: . . . and attempt to show that in the present era, and most recently in particular, it has become applicable to the broad masses, who certainly do not put the intellectual ego, subjectively erected into the 'real' world, in the place of God, . . .

Lukács: Yes . . .

Kofler: . . . but rather consumption, free time, etc., although in the manipulated sense which we already spoke of a while ago. On this kind of basis we can point for example—without being able to deal fully here with the connecting links—to the despiritualization of the masses, which has proceeded so far that even the traditionally rooted religious consciousness, which Marx alluded to, has been dissolved earlier than Marx had foreseen, before the advent of classless society, and for contrary reasons. Here we are also dealing with a kind of religious atheism, one form of which is perhaps that today the churches are at times quite full, but in part full of atheists. At the same time we can observe in great detail quite remarkable lapses into magic. Magic substitutes for the original religion insofar as, for example, attempts to influence fate by means of the pools and astrology are to be classified, in view of modern rationality, as quasi-religious or magical myths. Attempts to create a value for life by means of drugs belongs here also. I am thinking now of LSD, which has become so famous. We must take these things all the more seriously, in view of the fact that a book glorifying narcotics has been written by the philosopher Huxley.

Lukács: I know it . . .

Kofler: You know it? What don't you know, Herr Lukács? I thought I was giving you information which you were not familiar with. In this book, *The Doors of Perception*, Huxley creates a mythological ideology of a 'new way', a mythology of salvation of a purely subjective kind, a salvation forced and mediated by narcotics. It is most disturbing that such people as Leary, the well-known Harvard psychologist, are founding colonies for training people in the 'transcendental life', that there have in fact been theologists like Professor Clark, for example, who has carried out experiments with theology students —with theology students, I emphasize—with the result that students and theologists maintained they had got nearer to God —Clark's own words—by means of LSD.

Lukács: Correct.

Kofler: If you pursue these things still further, you discover a remarkable process, whose dialectic might be defined as the employment of magical forms of orgiastic ecstasy for the solution of modern human problems; remember for example the ecstatic, convulsive phenomena of the Beatles performances. In connection with this withdrawal into the privacy of the ego, a new god is created, a new quasi-religious consciousness, as a result of the inability of the ego to live itself out at work, in public and social life, since it is there suppressed. In the final analysis we are faced here with a new, quite modern form of irrationalism and religious atheism, whose study and analysis is of the greatest significance for Marxism today, which I believe is now developing further than ever.

Lukács: I think you are completely right. You will excuse me however if I divide your question, which you have treated as a whole, into two separate parts. The first part would be a general history of the transformations, through struggle, of the economic formations in which we find ourselves today. It is illusory to believe that these developments, and in particular the development of the subjective factor within them, follow a rectilinear pattern. To consider only religious phenomena: in the late Middle Ages and the Renaissance religion faded into a kind of enlightened indifference, only to flare up into a fervour with the peasant wars and the Reformation, which in the previous centuries was simply not conceivable. The following is an opinion of mine, which I regard as very important in this connection. At the end of the nineteenth century, in the second half of the nineteenth century, the class struggle was on the whole constantly sharpening, and reached a peak during the First World War and in 1917. After World War Two, however, new conditions brought about a quite different situation, and our young people, who are, I would say, impatient, the angry young people of the left, are falling into certain Chinese temptations, since for them the development is not going quickly enough—people dream of a revolution in the U.S.A. tomorrow, or they want to travel to South America and become guerillas. Our concern as Marxists should be to come to a clear understanding of everything that has happened since the close of the first great period. We should analyse how this transformation of capitalism into a form dominated by relative surplus value has created a new situation in which the workers' movement, the revolutionary movement, is condemned to a new beginning, and in which such apparently long superseded ideologies as the machine-wrecking of the end of the eighteenth century are experiencing a renaissance. Perhaps it will sound paradoxical to you if I see in this great 'sex wave', which today even involves women and young girls, an equivalent of machine-wrecking in the battle for female independence. At first sight this may seem a paradox, but I believe that something like this is hidden in it.

Today, in arousing the subjective factor, we cannot recreate and continue the 1920s, we have instead to proceed on the basis of a new beginning, with all the experience that we have from the earlier workers' movement and from Marxism. We must be clear about this, however, that the problem is to begin anew; to use an analogy, we are not now in the twenties of the twentieth century, but in a certain sense at the beginning of the nineteenth century, when the workers' movement slowly began to take shape in the wake of the French Revolution. I believe that this idea is very important for theorists, for despair can very rapidly set in if the assertion of certain truths only finds a very weak resonance. Don't forget that certain things that Saint-Simon and Fourier spoke about had at the time an extraordinarily weak resonance, and it was only in the thirties and forties of the nineteenth century that a revival of the workers' movement got under way. Of course one should not stretch analogies too far, and analogies do not expand in parallel, but I believe you will understand what I mean if I say that we must come to a clear understanding that we find ourselves at the beginning of a new period, and that our duty as theorists is to make clear to people the possibilities open to humanity in this period, knowing that the resonance of this knowledge among the masses will be weak for the time being. This is naturally related to the Stalinist development in the Soviet Union, to the hesitant way in which it is being overcome and the later development of socialism resulting from it. Great events can have very negative effects on the subjective factor, and—to take once again a historic example—it was the heroic defeat of the left Jacobins in the French Revolution that gave rise to the utopian idea that socialism had nothing to do with the revolutionary movement. I believe that the cause of this was basically nothing other than disillusion with French developments in the years 1793 and 1794, but it had a very enduring effect on the workers' movement, and basically it was only Marx who asserted the central importance of the struggle for the democratic revolution as a step towards the struggle for socialism. Today, however, we have no political leaders capable of converting this knowledge into political practice. It was a completely unique case that we had in the 1917 period the remarkable combination of an important theorist and a great political leader in the person of Lenin, and it is by no means certain that we will have this unified form of politics in future. We have now the beginnings of the theory, but there is still no political leader on the horizon capable of converting this theory into political slogans; yet I am strongly convinced that as the movement grows stronger, these political leaders will also emerge.

In connection with this I now return to the second part of the question, the religious side. This is a very interesting problem, which has not been investigated by anyone at all, and in particular not by us Marxists, for dogmatic Marxism has not yet got beyond ideas about religion that date from the forties of the nineteenth century. One used to read articles to the effect that the rockets that were sent up into space found no sign of God there, and there were atheists who imagined that an argument like this would work on anyone, as if there was even a washerwoman today who still believed in heaven in the sense of Thomas Aquinas or even of Dante's *Divine Comedy*. It is beyond question that the whole ontological basis of the old religion has broken down, and the ontological basis was always one of the decisive aspects. It is certainly not for the first time now, but basically ever since Schleiermacher's doctrine of 'absolute dependence', that religious people are faced with the necessity of simply putting aside the old religious ontology, and seeking some kind of new ontology for what I have termed in my *Aesthetic* the religious need. Now, what really is this religious need? It is a man's gloomy feeling that his life is not meaningful, and now, since he cannot find a direction in life by himself, since the old religious ontology has broken down—and certainly broken down in the sense that I believe there are neither Catholics nor Protestants today who would take the Old and New Testaments as the historical and ontological foundation of their behaviour—

now these people too stand before the void, and what you very correctly say amounts to magic is nothing other than the attempt to find a new basis, in the face of this standing-in-empty-space. This shows that the problem of a meaningful life, which I have raised with regard to the manipulated world of capitalism in a Marxist sense, is basically the same problem that the religious need faces today, and we must look for a point of insertion here.

In this search we come up against two obstacles. The first of these is the dogmatic conception of many Marxists, who think in terms of the old arguments for atheism which have today lost any effectiveness. On the other hand it is no accident that people like Garaudy are seeking to find a common ideological ground with figures such as Teilhard de Chardin, to take an example. Naturally there can be no true convergence, and we cannot lend a hand to these people, whose religious need is genuine but who seek ideologically false props for it, by recognizing their false props. The question here is a very complicated one for Marxism, and I would indicate it by pointing out that it is no accident that the young Marx wrote his doctoral dissertation on Epicurus. For the Epicurean philosophy, in which the gods live in the spaces between worlds, means that god, the godly, the transcendental principle, has and can have no influence on human life, that man must therefore come to terms with the fact that he alone can give himself a meaningful life, and that in this struggle for a meaningful life, as the *Internationale* puts it, 'No saviours from on high deliver'—this is the point at which we must seek to transform religious atheism into real atheism. This raises a whole series of philosophical problems, and I would like to draw attention here, as in many other particular questions, to the work of Nikolai Hartmann, who in his little book on teleology pointed out that man experiences the events of his everyday life as a teleology directed independently of him. If for example someone near to you has died, you ask, 'Why does this happen to me?', as if the death of X Y was teleologically ordained in order to affect the moral life of Z. Here, in my opinion, is the decisive point in the construction of Marxism, the Epicurean dialectic with which we could help enlighten these religious atheists.

Without doubt all churches now find themselves in an ideological crisis, which could be compared with the great ideological crisis of the Reformation. I would say here that the crisis of the Reformation in the Catholic domain arose through the Catholic church being adapted purely to the support of feudalism; Loyola's great achievement, after the crisis, was precisely to recognize that the Catholic church could only sustain itself as a church, and expand, in alliance with the rising capitalism. Now we find ourselves in a crisis in which the Catholic and other churches are beginning to realize that this life-and-death alliance with capitalism is something dangerous. I believe that the present crisis will be handled more diplomatically; Pope John XXIII has apparently seen clearly enough that this one-sided orientation to the religious support of capitalism must be given up and a new orientation sought. I am speaking by analogy with Loyola in the seventeenth century. So to answer the second question: our analysis of the present religious need must be neither dogmatic nor ideologically indulgent, for we can only begin to give help to those who find themselves today in this religious crisis insofar as we are struggling in the most diverse ways to make possible a meaningful life, and to form an alliance including, as its third element, those Marxists in the socialist countries who are attempting to liquidate Stalinism; for those tendencies that make life meaningful can only be realized today in these countries on the basis of the liquidation of Stalinism. Other things being equal, they should have emerged earlier and more clearly under socialism than under capitalism, but they have been held back by the Stalinist system and by the Stalinist manner in which it has so far been superseded. I do not know whether it is clear to you that very different forces are at work here, in very complicated ways; we will fall into illusions if we expect the struggle against manipulation to yield any kind of spectacular results. The most important thing, for the time being, is to attain complete theoretical clarity as to what Marxism signifies today and what it can achieve.

Kofler: Three things have struck me in your detailed and many-levelled presentation. I would just like to raise one as a problem for discussion, although I would first like to at least indicate the existence of the other two. Your epistemological and anthropological explanation of religion, as it were, still has to be properly related to Marx's definition of religion as a 'sigh of the oppressed creature'. It struck me both in the first and second volumes of your *Aesthetic* that you deal at great length with the problem of religion, without really demonstrating this connection, but I believe we need not discuss this here. I would further like to point out that the 'machine-wrecking' of women and girls that you mentioned is, strange to say, tolerated to a surprising degree, indeed even promoted, and in this connection I submit the question, why exactly? The suspicion that arises here is whether this form of rebellion against traditional taboos does not in fact precisely ensure the success of the integrative tendency, in a remarkably intricate dialectic.

Lukács: Look here, I believe you are quite right. If we compare sexuality with machine-wrecking, then the comparison bears on the human motivation behind it, and not on the movement itself. Machine-wrecking could not be integrated into the capitalism of that time, but these unclear ideological movements can be very well integrated. A very interesting example can be introduced here. Mannheim, in his celebrated book, is extraordinarily harsh towards ideology, while he has a certain excusable weakness, a charming indulgence, towards utopia. Because there is no room for revolutionary praxis in this division between ideology and utopia—a utopia can, as you say, be very well integrated as a utopia—an opposition which has such distant goals that their realization is impossible in principle is very susceptible to being integrated by a capitalism of the present type. I know exactly why certain things are acceptable and certain things are not. For example, when Ernst Bloch, to name a serious philosopher, said that even nature would change under socialism, this was something which no one had any objection to, and hence Bloch could be a distinguished and recognized philosopher, although his socialism was so radical that it even changed nature. If I say on the other hand that there is a connection between Nietzsche and Hitler, then I am already an 'official spokesman' or I don't know what, who is undermining the holiest traditions of the German mind, for a critique of Nietzsche vitally affects contemporary nationalism. You will excuse me for taking a personal example, but it just shows—and this is very essential for extending the struggle against manipulation—that sometimes extraordinarily radical things can be acknowledged as interesting points of view, while quite simple matters that appear quite prosaic are condemned as—how shall I say—restricted or dogmatic or obsolescent or I don't know what. One must be quite clear today about this situation.

Kofler: Other personal examples could be mentioned of course, not only those concerning Bloch . . .

Lukács: May I say here that I brought in Bloch because I consider him the best man. One could take many, many stronger cases involving others. But one cannot doubt Bloch's integrity, nor his ability, and what I would say here is that *even* Bloch was accepted in this way, others naturally to a far greater extent.

Kofler: There are, however, schools that produce great numbers of these angry young people, as you called them, who certainly do not want to go to Vietnam to fight, but who in their anger take up a position that is partly revolutionary and one of anti-capitalist enlightenment, but also partly one of resignation. It is quite often said that this is the tendency in Frankfurt. And here I come to another problem, which is at the same time a problem in your own writing, and that is the problem of those people who are not merely angry, and not those who, despite their criticism, still somehow resignedly adapt, but the problem of the 'positive examples'. In your book on the German realists, where you discuss Gottfried Keller, you say something like this: certain tendencies of Keller's art have great significance, pointing far into the future, presenting us with truly exemplary figures of a democratic life, so that the real human and democratic traits of any genuine democracy take on an ideal form before our eyes, without realism being thereby abandoned. This certainly happens in a remarkable way, which we cannot discuss here, but you expressly emphasize, 'without realism being abandoned'. The question here is one of true examples, and it is this which I would particularly like to dwell on. 'Without realism being abandoned', in other words, without falling into an abstruse utopia! But does this not also mean that these figures which embody a really human democracy must even be found in present-day life? Following from this, are these figures at all detectable in the totally deformed and fetishized life that is characteristic of our era? And if to a certain extent . . . Excuse me . . .

Lukács: Yes . . .

Kofler: . . . if the subtle methods of repressive integration still remain dominant, are we not simply speaking with the voice of a utopian ideology, which certainly serves its purpose, in a certain fashion, but perhaps overlooks the whole process, misses it? I would particularly like to underline that this is not my own question. These were questions which I brought with me to put to you.

Lukács: I would like to say that the formation of a conscious minority is the precondition of a mass movement. In my opinion, Lenin described this very well in *What is to be Done?* Returning to the example of Keller, I will not choose a central theme of his to discuss but rather a small matter where the distinction can be clearly made. Take the short story *Frau Regel Amrain* for the problem of education. It is a remarkable fact that Frau Amrain shows her son the greatest indulgence in all cases where he has behaved, so to speak, badly or naughtily, and only intervenes vigorously when he does something really base. Here for example is a case of exemplary behaviour, which is in no way changed by the fact that Frau Regel Amrain belongs to a foundering Swiss society. Realism is always portrayal, and here it is precisely this foundering society that is portrayed. Nevertheless this moral problem of the struggle against baseness and degradation is a valid one, a problem that plays a great role, for example, in our own struggle against manipulation. This is absolutely possible even today.

I will take another contemporary example, Jorge Semprun's novel *The Long Voyage*, which contains some very significant things. You spoke of the present situation and the literature portraying it. I find it really a little disgraceful for literature, if I consider the entire literature of the last twenty years, that this wonderful book published in the 1950s, with the last letters of the antifascists condemned to death, which shows such a profusion of human greatness, bravery and resistance, has given writers no impulse. Semprun's book is really one of the first books in which literature begins to approach the human level of these letters, which was already realized in true life. I am not saying that there is nothing similar; there is the fine short story by Hochhuth, *The Berlin Antigone*, and there are very good things in Böll's *Billiards at Half past Nine*. You understand, I am not talking now about artistic things, I am talking now about life. The old woman in Böll's story, who is shut up in a lunatic asylum and finally takes a shot at the soldiers in blind rage, is a genuine figure of protest against fascism and a gesture towards its spiritual liquidation, in contrast to what is happening today in Germany. And now there is something in Semprun's work which I should very much like to draw attention to, concerning as it does one particular aspect of that dreadful episode that was fascism, the Jewish question, which in any case cannot be depicted often enough as an example of brutal manipulation. Nevertheless I consider it wrong to reduce the superseding of fascism to the Jewish question as is the present tendency in Germany. It is only one aspect of fascism, and Semprun has portrayed the matter very finely, and also very bravely, as a Jewish self-criticism. One of his characters in particular is a German Jewish communist, who comes to France, fights with the French partisans, and falls as a partisan, and Semprun writes concerning him, 'I will not die a Jewish death'. The Jewish death was that hundreds of thousands, millions, were thrown into the gas ovens without making the least attempt at any kind of resistance. The Warsaw ghetto uprising was really something of this kind, but I believe that if you compare reality with literature, even literature about the Jews, then this Jewish communist partisan who falls in France is the first figure in literature who stands at the level of the Warsaw uprising. I don't know whether it is clear to you what I mean by this, and that literature has a great task here. I have also referred to the same thing in a quite different context. If you compare Solzhenitsyn's novel *One Day in the Life of Ivan Denisovitch* with the rest of the concentration-camp novels, you have a great division between, on the one hand, a naturalistic description of atrocities, and on the other hand, the problem as to in what ways, by cunning or whatever, a man in a camp can preserve his human integrity. It is in this regard that Solzhenitsyn's novel is something new and something revolutionary. This is the way in which literature could make an extraordinary contribution to the struggle against manipulation, i.e. by refusing to capitulate in the face of manipulation and to consider manipulation as destiny. I have deliberately brought in these examples to show that it is possible in the field of *belles lettres* to portray these real revolts, which you find in the last letters of the antifascists condemned to death, either using present-day means and present-day events, or by going back to the old events, in an exemplary way for the action of contemporary men in the struggle against manipulation. It is beyond question that such a literature exists. There is for example this very interesting novel by the American William Styron, *Lie Down in Darkness*, which combines the phenomena of manipulation into a great explosive human tragedy, in the manner of Dostoyevsky. On the one hand he shows how the rich man cannot avoid becoming a manipulating tyrant, and the poor man a sacrifice to this manipulation, and after he has shown this, he portrays the uprising of the poor man against his manipulated condition in a murder, which is ultimately committed as a personal protest. On the other hand the book is very interesting for the idea that the murderer manages to avoid the consequences of his act through fortunate circumstances, and afterwards leads a contented and meaningful life. Obviously more examples could be added, although such works are few and far between. I simply believe that we should not fall into pessimism because of the present weakness of the movement against manipulation. We have opportunities, we have allies, and I believe there are very many people who are inwardly discontented, as you can imagine, and it is theoretical and artistic clarity that will now determine in what manner and at what pace we will be able to carry out our task.

Kofler: Your point about capitulation in the face of manipulation reminds me of the passage in your analysis of Thomas Mann, in connection with Raabe, where you speak of peripheral heroes . . .

Lukács: Yes . . .

Kofler: . . . peripheral heroes or peripheral figures, who vainly seek through struggle to break through to the wide world outside.

Lukács: Yes . . .

Kofler: The result is human distortion—I would say in regard to the contemporary world, sectarianism. We have quite a lot of figures like this in our time, who take extraordinary pains to achieve this breakthrough . . .

Lukács: Yes . . .

Kofler: . . . but who remain trapped in their own dreams . . .

Lukács: Yes . . .

Kofler: . . . since they dogmatically misconstrue historical changes, and then reproach others with betrayal . . .

Lukács: Yes . . .

Kofler: . . . or alternatively, they attempt to extract from the bourgeois life-situation of late capitalism something like a human life for themselves, a human democratization . . .

Lukács: Yes . . .

Kofler: . . . and finally resign themselves and exhibit just the same human distortion as their ostensible opposites.

Lukács: Yes . . .

71

Kofler: The question now arises, whether sectarianism is not symptomatic of a time of crisis, in which something new is nevertheless happening; in the first place, is this dissipation of subjectively progressive forces, which are as much of bourgeois as of socialist provenance, not a necessity explicable in terms of the critical situation of the progressive forces, and in the second place, does not sectarianism after all contain the possibility of historical effectiveness in the future, so that something positive could still come out of it that could perhaps even be identified in anticipation in the perspective of historical theory? This is how the problem of peripheral heroes or peripheral figures appears to me in the present epoch.

Lukács: The less a really major movement has arisen, the more positive is the value that even errors can have for its development. Today we can see quite clearly that Fourier's conception, according to which labour was to be transformed into a kind of play, was completely false. Despite this, in the circumstances of that time, when capitalist labour was being blindly extolled, this utopian attitude of Fourier's, which by the way already surfaced before Fourier, in Schiller's aesthetic, was of positive significance. It only acquired a negative significance when Marx discovered the correct way forward. Obviously the most varied attempts that are genuinely directed against contemporary manipulation have a positive tendency—I do not include all attempts. I have still not read the article in question, but it is very interesting that the last number of *Temps Modernes* put forward for discussion a critical attack on Teilhard de Chardin as an ideologist of manipulation. There is in fact a very close connection between Teilhard de Chardin's conceptions and—how should I say—this neopositivist world outlook of manipulation. I would say once more with Hegel that the truth is concrete and that there can be sectarians who in a certain sense point positively towards the future, while there can also be sectarians whose effect is negative even today.

Kofler: Herr Lukács, I don't want to overburden you, but perhaps I might put you one further question, which is at the same time linked to a critical remark which greatly occupied the seminar that I lead. In the first half-volume of your *Aesthetic*, in connection with the question of reflection, you speak of the unity of reality.

Lukács: Yes ...

Kofler: We already touched on this question yesterday, and now the following problem arises. In your *History and Class Consciousness* of 1923, you demonstrated how classical philosophy relates the cognizability of reality to the 'production' of this reality. In your criticism of this philosophy you rightly reproached it with failing to see that the problem of the cognizability of the real world can only be solved on the basis of the concept of social praxis. This problem remains insoluble, unless the concept of praxis is introduced. Here then is the question: Do not the two concepts of production, i.e. the epistemological and the social, refer to two different realms of reality, the latter to the sphere of material production, as it were, while the former refers to the object of natural science and mathematics. Your argument can be read as if there was no breach between the two, but this can perhaps be criticized from the standpoint that two concepts of production are really operating here.

Lukács: To start with I must say immediately that, as you probably know, I regard *History and Class Consciousness* as a superseded book, and this argument in *History and Class Consciousness* thus has nothing to do with the problems developed in the *Aesthetic*. Now as to what unity of reality and production mean, reality is unitary in the sense that all real phenomena—whether they be inorganic, organic or social—occur in definite complexes according to definite causal sequences, with reciprocal action both within and between these complexes. This identity is given. I believe, however, as I already tried to demonstrate in my book on Hegel, that one of the most important innovations that Hegel introduced into the dialectic consisted in taking, as its fundamental principle, not the unity of opposites, but rather what Hegel calls the identity of identity and non-identity. Now I believe that there is a unitary reality, an identity that consists

of a causal progression independent of all human projects—
I will come back to this directly. It then follows, firstly, that this
unity manifests itself in the three different forms of reality in
different ways. Production as it occurs in labour consists of course
in the labourer setting himself a teleological aim that he plans to
realize. In this way something completely new can come into
being. One need in no way look so far afield as atomic science.
There is essentially no such thing as a wheel in nature as we
know it, whereas men came to produce the wheel at a relatively
early stage in their development. The nature of the teleological
project is such that, with the help of the knowledge of causal
series, it allows these precise causal series in nature to act on one
another in a different combination than would have occurred
without the teleological project. However the existing causal
relationships can only be known and applied; they can never be
altered. Hegel says quite correctly about labour in his early
writings that man with his tools lets nature toil on itself. This
production thus involves an identity of identity and non-
identity, insofar as the wheel is certainly something newly produced by men, but yet there is nothing in the wheel that does not
correspond exactly to the prevailing causal series in nature that
are independent of men. Man would not have been able to create
the wheel if he had not in a certain sense recognized this, and
this production is thus a complicated process which does not
contradict the unity of reality.

If I now come back to this unity of reality in its higher forms,
I mean by this something which we have spoken about earlier
with regard to the question of religion, that, for example, nature
—organic as much as inorganic nature—runs its course and
passes away according to its own dialectic, independent of the
teleological projects of men. The psychological endowment of a
man, just as his physiological constitution, is accidental, as far as
society is concerned. I believe Marx once said correctly in this
regard that it is accidental what men a revolutionary situation
chances upon as leaders of the working class, although this
already is no longer a purely physiological or psychological

matter. Nevertheless there remains here an insuperable element of chance, which arises precisely from the purely causal development of natural occurrences. In this connection human praxis confronts a unitary nature, and if I practise any kind of social activity, including the cognition of natural laws, of human psychology and so on, there are lawful processes at work in this complex which I cannot transcend. I can exert a definite transforming influence on external reality on the basis of my knowledge, but the laws of this reality are effective without me, and in this respect I confront, as economic producer, as artist or as philosopher, a unitary reality, whose unitariness must again be understood in the sense of an identity of identity and non-identity.

Kofler: How does Marx's assertion in the *Economic and Philosophic Manuscripts* that nature is nothing without men stand in this connection?

Lukács: If I were to say that nature, from which man has developed as a consequence of various accidents, would in this sense be nothing without him, then I would make this splendid aphorism into a triviality. But Marx certainly did not mean that the Earth owes its existence to the fact that man is active on it, and that, if there are no men living on Venus and Mars, then Venus and Mars do not exist. I believe that we are dealing here with a paradoxical formulation of the young Marx, who was concerned to draw out the further consequences of the Epicurean idea of necessity. For if the gods live in an intermundane space, this also means that men can only have a transforming effect on nature in the context of human praxis and that nature moreover evidently develops completely independently of men. I do not believe that Marx would have departed from this conception.

Kofler: Certainly, this is how it should be understood. I would like to return now to the original source of the question, in order to make one final remark. Hegel relates the production of reality by mind—of course an absolute mind—to the problem of production in society, as if these elements were on the same level.

Is it not necessary to make a division here, so that there are no mistakes and no misunderstandings?

Lukács: You see, I would like to say about this that I am very sceptical about the great importance of epistemological problems. I am afraid that epistemological problems, if they are not treated as an aspect of ontological ones, distort things and make similarities where there are no similarities, and dissimilarity where there is similarity. One must be extraordinarily careful with epistemology. I will simply mention one important case in point. For Kant the distinction between appearance and essence in what is for us the real world vanishes, for according to Kant's theory the world given to us is only an appearance, with a transcendental unknowable thing-in-itself behind it. For Hegel on the other hand reality consists both of a really existing essence and of a world of appearance which is itself real. This already shows that one can establish a tradition only by means of ontology, and in speaking of production in the Marxist sense, this can only be taken to mean the products of labour, in the broadest sense; production arises as . . .

Kofler: Social production . . .

Lukács: Well yes, of course, but social production develops from the extension of the division of labour, as a result of the ever more complicated teleological projects which are built up on the primary teleological project and form an unprecedented system. If anyone analysed society completely into its component parts, he would arrive, I believe, at the single teleological project as the atom from which society is built up. This synthesis, however, has not arisen teleologically. Every single purchase and sale of commodities, for example, is at the time a teleological project. It is a teleological project when a woman goes to the market and buys five pears. In the market, however, the thousand teleological projects give rise to a market causality, which connects up with other market causalities, so that the individual teleological projects are effective only in their causal product. It is the insuperable aspect of objectivity and lawfulness in social existence, that the outcome of the individual teleological projects which it consists of presents a quite different aspect to that which was intended in them . . .

Kofler: We spoke of this yesterday . . .

Lukács: For example, the average rate of profit arises out of the quest for surplus profit; the quest for surplus profit is certainly a mark of the individual project, and can even be successful in the individual case, but in the total development the average profit nevertheless appears as a feature of the total process. Philosophic investigation of the problems of freedom and necessity in society must start from this nucleus. It would be a very important contribution to this, in my opinion, to deal with causality and teleology independently of one another, as two co-existing forms of determinacy, and this problem has not been sufficiently considered in philosophy. There was a time when teleology was simply denied; in fact, however, one should say that in itself and independently, there exists only causality; in social existence teleological projection is added, but a teleological project can only be present in a causally determined world. Here you can see what I meant earlier when I said that epistemologically, I can analyse causality and teleology as independent relations. If I begin to analyse things ontologically, however, I see things that apparently contradict one another. On the one hand, teleology is only possible under the dominance of causality, while on the other hand new objects, forms and connections arise in society only as a consequence of teleological projects. From an epistemological standpoint this seems very paradoxical, but if you consider it ontologically, it is a simple analysis of the labour project.

Kofler: Quite right. I only made my interjection so that new misunderstandings should not arise in connection with the concept of production.

Lukács: . . . Yes, yes . . .

Kofler: . . . passing on, I wonder whether you understand by this only labour . . .

Lukács: I believe that the labour project . . .

Kofler: . . . is primary.

Lukács: You see, the concept of coordination, for example, develops from the labour project. So does the concept of intellectual preparation for labour, and so on. If this process develops further into a social division of labour, then tradition arises, and the consequences related to it. At a further stage law arises, and any legal project is also a teleological project, any legal project consists in my saying: I want Franz Müller imprisoned for three months because he stole two cartons. There can be no legal proposition that does not itself contain either a teleological project or a derivation of one or more teleological projects. I believe that we cannot ignore the fact of teleological projection, right up to the highest forms of science and art.

Kofler: If you speak of ontology, do you not really mean anthropology?

Lukács: No, because I believe that certain ontological constellations exist completely independently of whether any human being is present. If, for example, I investigate the possibility of organic life on the various planets in our solar system, then that has nothing to do with human beings. For it does not necessarily follow from the fact that life will develop on a planet that this life has to lead to man. Here there is a second leap involved, which we cannot analyse for lack of material, but I am firmly convinced that further analysis will lead to some very complicated results. Marx quite correctly saw that Darwinism settled accounts with teleology. And we can already see today that there are blind alleys in the development of living species, and indeed at relatively high stages of development. The highest forms of so-called animal society are to be found among the insects, not among the higher animals, and it is precisely the social nature of insects that limits their further development. Since the division of labour among the bees, for example, is a biological one, the beehive can only undergo biological changes, it cannot develop from the queen's rule into a democracy—I deliberately bring up this old chestnut here. For further social development is only possible in that constellation which is exclusively present in the human species, in which the division of labour has a social and not a biological character.

Kofler: Certainly, but is it not different in traditional philosophy? Whatever one could accept in this point, in the realm of human society everything is still different, i.e. anthropological. For example, if a philosophy is made up out of the concept of teleology, then philosophy is perhaps shifted onto an area where it leads to false problems and false solutions.

Lukács: There is of course today a very strong tendency to reduce this question to anthropology. But this reduction leaves out of account the entire past of nature, and thus leaves out certain things in human life also that happen only as a result of inorganic necessity. For example, a clever man once drew my attention to the interesting fact that there is no single living species which has an odd number of locomotive organs. There are certain things which we have odd numbers of—we have one nose and one mouth. But we have two feet, and you will not be able to name a single species that has three feet or five feet; they all have two feet, four feet, eight feet, ten feet, etc., and this is simply a function of the physical laws of motion, which living species have obeyed in this fashion. Should I call this anthropology? I believe this would be a slightly excessive extension of the term.

I believe that the stress on anthropology follows from an attitude that I regard as correct and progressive, i.e. that people have come to doubt what the so-called science of psychology really is. Psychology has isolated certain modes of human expression and not seen in doing so that every such mode is the resultant of a double causality, conditioned on the one hand by human physiology and the effects of these physiological forces, on the other hand by man's reaction to what happens in society. Psychology confines itself to the one unified expression. If I say for example that a smell is offensive to me, this is already no longer purely physiological, for you know how many smells are subject to fashion and how extremely socially determined it is in what way people react to certain smells. This is perhaps not a good example; I only want to show that there is no single so-called psychological reaction which is not simultaneously and

79

inseparably both physiological and social. I would not exclude the possibility that in time a science of anthropology may be constructed which would concentrate on the interaction of these two components. It is illusory, however, to believe that fundamental problems of social development will be thereby resolvable, for social development, although it involves men, develops on the basis of the specific laws of the economy. And I would be very curious to see, to return to my earlier example, how the falling rate of profit could be derived anthropologically.

Kofler: I think we could get into an endless discussion here. Thank you very much, Herr Lukács, for your patience.

Third Conversation

Georg Lukács—Wolfgang Abendroth

Elements for a Scientific Politics

Abendroth: Herr Lukács, yesterday you explained to us that the essential difference between modern late-capitalist industrial society and the previous period consisted in the central issue of class conflict shifting from absolute to relative surplus value. I don't need to go over the reasons for this again. And you drew the further conclusion that the problem of progress has largely come to take the form of a struggle for genuine free time, time that is no longer manipulated—the question is how the reduction in working time is to be utilized. I regard this as completely convincing and correct, although of course the struggle for higher wages still plays a role in the late-capitalist countries, and can come to the fore again in recessions. Now a whole series of problems arises in this connection. I am not certain that we assess them differently, but they should nevertheless be clearly formulated. You know that the dominant bourgeois sociology, including neo-positivist sociology, concludes from observing the external phenomena of this question that the class struggle is basically at a complete end and has now in fact vanished, because it sees the class struggle only as a struggle over absolute surplus value. The sociologists assume that in consequence of this the working class, a working class enlarged by broader strata—in particular salaried employees—has ceased to be the subject of the struggle for progress. Do you share this opinion?

Lukács: No, of course not. In the first place I believe that, if you take the condition of the present-day working class, objective analysis shows that this idea is quite incorrect. We can indeed observe the world over an undoubted regression of working-class consciousness. This regression of consciousness, the decline of the subjective factor, has found its truest expression on the world scale in the form of social democracy, which has not only turned against socialism, as in 1917, but is now so completely committed to manipulated democracy that today you can barely distinguish a speech of a German Social Democrat from a speech of a CDU member. Present-day social democracy is thus characterized not only by its resistance to socialism, but by its abandonment of any democracy worthy of the name. The problem of a social democratization, of a real democratic development, scarcely retains any significance for the SPD. This can be minutely observed, from the emergency laws through to the debates on defence. The ideals of genuine democracy were once pursued very energetically by certain of the old-style social democrats—just think of the position taken by Jaurès at the time of the Dreyfus trial—but they no longer mean anything to the SPD, they have almost completely vanished. Yet the economic class struggle has quite clearly not come to an end, and it is an interesting symptom that the trade unions, or at least a section of the trade unions, generally stand to the left of the social-democratic parties, which was never the case in the earlier movement. The idea that the working class has ceased to be a vehicle of struggle against capitalist forms of exploitation is thus false. All that can be said is that we are in a trough of consciousness in this respect, and things like this are always changeable.

At the same time it is undoubtedly true that completely new problems have come to the forefront of the movement, in the shape of the problems of free time and of leisure. Earlier struggles over free time only went as far as to campaign for working hours that permitted the workers some kind of human existence. Today there is much more involved. In fact through the shortening of working hours a space arises in which free time can be turned into real leisure. But present-day capitalism does everything to prevent this. This is not fundamentally for ideological reasons, but simply because the manipulated marketing of the consumer goods industries is necessarily linked with a conformist ideology of enjoyment. Now in my opinion this gives rise to completely new problems, which are not just directly generated by the economic structure of the society. They show rather the necessity of the transition to socialism and form a qualitatively new element in social development. Any economic and social movement is always based on the individual teleological projects of human beings. It is in the first instance quite immaterial whether economic, scientific or moral projects are involved. Teleological projects are always conceived in the mind, and a project only becomes real when the attempt is made to put it into practice in the material world. But the overall structure of societies up till now has always arisen, as Marx very rightly said, behind men's backs. Forms of human social life, such as the polis, feudalism or capitalism, were dictated to by men by economic development, and men only then reacted on them in their teleological projects. In these contemporary questions about the utilization of free time the first problem that arises is that the economy is not in a position here to dictate the content of teleological projects; men themselves have to decide. I will give some examples.

There is now this great record industry and the spread of music. As far as the manipulator is concerned, it is all one and the same whether someone buys jazz or a Beethoven sonata. He will not manipulate someone into buying only jazz, and you can see from statistics that classical works also have their best-sellers. In this connection there is thus no direct manipulation in favour of bad culture. Men have to make decisions here with relative autonomy. It is in the same sense, on the broader scale of the economy in general, that socialism involves a leap forward from hitherto-existing class society, for socialism makes its entry with the demand to subordinate the whole economy to the teleological projects of human consciousness. This is a completely new moment in history, and it is nothing to wonder at that men who have been accustomed for centuries to a different mode of existence find the transition to this new development very difficult, all the more so as there are very tempting forms of transition which are at first very efficient, in the economic sense.

So long as absolute surplus value prevails, then—except when capitalist society is directly threatened by revolution—individual capitalists or capitalist groups operate on the basis of immediately discernible exploitation. But once mass consumption has become central to capitalist reproduction, as a consequence of relative surplus value, capitalism acquires an interest in this mass consumption; capital as a whole has something like a direct interest in a relatively high standard of living for the masses. I am not saying that this is immediately achieved. But if you take phenomena such as Roosevelt, or to a lesser degree Kennedy, you see what distinguishes them from the others. They are not just representatives of particular capitalist lobbies, but rather attempt to promote the interests of capital as a whole. This is of course not planned theoretically, nor is it carried out practically in a consistent way. All I mean is that in all these things, in the relation of the individual man to his economic basis and to the ideological consequences of this situation, we find ourselves in a state of transition. Because of the long period of Stalinist rule and the reaction that this development produced, even in the capitalist world, Marxism is not yet developed enough to give clear and scientifically founded answers to these new questions. We Marxists are faced today with the task of solving these new problems theoretically and attempting to extract from this theoretical work new points of reference for practical responses.

Abendroth: I would agree with you on this. Only it seems to me that we must recognize an aspect of this progress that makes our situation unprecedentedly difficult. As long as the class struggle was based almost exclusively on the struggle over absolute surplus value, the identity between the working-class interest, on the one hand, and the interest of the struggle against capitalism and for its transformation into a new society on the other, was visible to anyone almost by direct experience. In the new situation this direct identity no longer seems to obtain, and the formation of class consciousness is made terribly difficult. This is particularly the case insofar as the manipulation of free time, the consumer goods industry, constantly reduces the mental abilities of the great majority of the population, in the area of literature for example. The reason for this is quite simple, and requires no conscious or direct political manipulation on the part of the managers of late capitalism; it is simply that higher turnover holds out the prospect of higher profit. The profit motive, which governs any capitalist society, requires late capitalism to adapt itself continually to the lowest possible mental level, to keep this level down or even reduce it further. Springer's *Bild Zeitung* is a typical example. In this way this lowest possible level is maintained or, what is more likely, the mental level of the broad masses is even ever further reduced.

The need for social reconstruction, however, demands mental autonomy. It can scarcely be doubted that the worker of the end of the last century or the beginning of our own was not yet so subordinated to this pressure from the consumer goods industry. He had on this account, and despite worse formal education, greater opportunity for independent thought than the worker of today. The achievement of class consciousness is thus made more difficult. However the trade unions must retain a residue of class ideas if they are to exist at all. They must therefore understand that no trade-union struggle is possible which is not also a cultural struggle and occasionally also a political struggle for the maintenance of cultural freedom. This is the basis of the remarkable new tendency in all capitalist countries for the trade-union movement to be generally more radical than those political parties that once represented working-class interests, but have since been integrated into the system. The social-democratic parties have declined into institutions that want, just like the other parties, to manipulate the broad masses and administer their voting strength in politics. They also seek, like the consumer goods industry, to appeal to the lowest possible mental level, and to keep this mental level down in the interest of their own manipulation. The debasement of social-democratic parties such as the SPD does not have to be explained in terms of conscious and direct betrayal by the leadership, but follows quite simply from this situation.

The central problem consequently becomes how we can

develop critical consciousness in this complicated situation. The worker himself can scarcely obtain a clear perspective from his own direct experience; the abstract thought of educated specialists is necessary for this. In the most developed industrial countries autonomous movements of intellectuals have a growing importance, movements which criticize a state power which is constantly becoming more authoritarian, the imperialist and neo-colonial policies of governments, and above all the manipulation of mental life, and thereby seek to uphold democratic and humanitarian traditions. In the United States this takes the form of the rebellion of students and young academics, who have engaged in struggle on behalf of the civil rights of coloured people and against the Vietnam policy. In the Federal Republic of Germany, which is most like the U.S.A. in its economic structure, socialist students and democratic writers and teachers have taken on a similar function. But they have so far largely failed to connect with the only class capable of really changing the situation, the working class. The critical intellectuals will only be able to achieve something, then, if they can once again mobilize this class, which forms the great majority of the population, against the powerful combination of the economic and political managers. Whether the so-called 'Western world' has a humanitarian future depends on this problem being solved. But will the critical intellectuals be able to solve it? The working class, both in the U.S.A. and the Federal Republic, is still in many respects lethargic, its consciousness manipulated; as long as economic stagnation or recession do not break the spell of apparent 'well-being', it will scarcely spontaneously produce the beginnings of new forms of class struggle and begin contesting mental manipulation and inhumanity. The isolated intellectuals are therefore all too frequently impatient and in danger of isolating themselves completely in a superficially radical subjectivism, before precise analysis of the situation provides them with the mental maturity, and changes in the economic situation the historic opportunity, to win the workers for struggle once more for their historic task. Can this not lead to a hopeless situation?

Lukács: Permit me to answer at this point, for you have raised so many questions that it is very difficult to pull them together. I generally do not like analogies very much, but there are nevertheless specific social situations in which certain things are repeated, not in details, but certainly in their strategic features. I already said on one of the previous days that in my opinion we are not in a position to correct the possible or real errors of the 1920s and build something up again on this basis. We are rather at a very primitive starting-point, characterized by movements of rebellion that are in some ways analogous to machine-wrecking, *mutatis mutandis*. What theoretical importance does this have? You are quite right to say that, in the era of absolute surplus value, the inclination of the working class to revolution was far greater than it is today. That is correct. But nonetheless, right through to Marx, the revolutionary theories of that time also did not grow directly out of the class struggle of the working class; Lenin was not wrong in maintaining, on the basis of a passage in Kautsky, that revolutionary theory is brought to the workers' movement from outside. We are of the opinion that today, when the objective situation is in many respects very, very unsatisfactory, more so than it was at an earlier stage of capitalism, the significance of this 'from outside' has increased extraordinarily. It is only from outside that class consciousness can be brought into the working class. And I believe that the intellectuals of today, the radical intellectuals, are faced with the great task of elaborating the principles and methods of this. I am talking here only of principles, not yet of the slogans that will grow out of these principles.

In this connection a point arises which is also in my opinion important, and which today we still underestimate, I believe on account of certain residues in our ideas, i.e. that the whole division between blue-collar and white-collar proletarians is precisely in the process of vanishing, as an objective economic division. I consider it a very important factor that earlier capitalism, capitalism before the great depression and the world wars, had an extraordinarily broad basis in a rentier stratum with a wealth of—let us say—two hundred thousand marks to six or seven hundred thousand marks. At that time there was a large section of intellectuals, university intellectuals in particular, who belonged to this rentier stratum by virtue of their private incomes, which gave them a material autonomy. This was the economic basis of Mannheim's free-floating intelligentsia. The new situation has now arisen that, partly because of the continuous devaluation of money, partly because of the constantly growing role of the intellectuals in manipulated capitalism, large sections of the rentier stratum have abandoned the capital which gave them a private income, and spent this money on the education of their children, so that this lower stratum of rentiers is in the process of dying out. I would not go so far as to say that it no longer exists. But essentially it has become more important for a man who was formerly in a position to save, say, five hundred thousand marks, to spend his entire income, partly on his own consumption, partly on the university education of his children. A very interesting side-effect of this, in my opinion, is that with this change, the one-child family is going out of fashion in France.

In France today there is a much greater increase in population than was formerly the case, which is perhaps related to the fact that the typical rentier of Maupassant's writings is in the process of dying out. This indicates a definite kinship between wage-workers and salaried employees in social life, even if this biological change is not yet apparent. The distinction between them, which was an important one in earlier capitalism, is steadily vanishing more and more completely, and I am firmly convinced that the disappearance of a distinction of this kind in social life will lead sooner or later to a change in consciousness. I only want to indicate by this that literature and art have endeavoured to portray this discontent with the contemporary manipulation of free time, and the inner emptiness of human existence. The popularity of a writer such as Beckett is related, in my opinion, to his way of portraying the complete meaninglessness of human life as a fatal destiny. This also shows where one has to apply oneself in order to set in motion the struggle against the world of manipulation. We must learn to link up with this discontent in various ways. Please allow me one more analogy with earlier times. Even in the heroic times of the working class of old, for example at the time of the struggle against the Anti-Socialist Law in Germany, etc., there were wide strata of the working class who read the *Gartenlaube*, went to church, and paid no heed to the class struggle. It would be illusory to believe that in this heroic period the entire working class participated in the heroic struggle. Not a word of it. And so I don't expect the strata that today still read *Bild Zeitung* and, as *Der Spiegel* once cleverly wrote, have plastic gnomes in their gardens, to make a direct leap from garden gnome to struggle against manipulation. On the other hand it can certainly not be ruled out that the start of some kind of mass movement against manipulation may come from those relatively broad strata among whom discontent is beginning to spread.

What forms this may take I cannot say. Unfortunately I am only a philosopher and not a politician; we could urgently do with a contemporary Lenin who could transform the position presently taken by Marxist theory into political action. Here I myself must abdicate and say that this lies outside my competence. It was a fortunate accident, but an uncommon one, for the proletarian movement to have had such successive figures as Marx, Engels and Lenin, who combined the two things. Today, however, this has the sad consequence that any first secretary of some party or other imagines himself to be a legitimate successor of Marx and Lenin. We must realize that this was a remarkable stroke of luck for the workers' movement, and that we can scarcely count on it being repeated. To take a really important example: I consider the late Togliatti one of the most talented tacticians that the workers' movement has produced. But I must also add that I do not value too highly Togliatti's theoretical compilations. Togliatti was a wonderful tactician, but no contemporary Lenin, and we should not regard him as such. On the other hand we should not wait for a Lenin, but rather attempt, insofar as it lies within our powers, to solve the combination of problems facing us. Theory can show in the first place what is new in social and economic phenomena. In my opinion, this is already a great deal. For these reflections already indicate that real economic phenomena are different from how bourgeois economics portrays them. Secondly, theory can draw conclusions from history which make the possibility of a movement credible —I would like to underline here the word 'movement'. I consider it illusory to expect a radical socialist party to arise immediately anywhere in the West. The problem is to create a movement which constantly puts this question on the agenda, which constantly mobilizes ever greater strata for the struggle against manipulation. It can certainly not be ruled out here that today's reader of Beckett will tomorrow become a fighter against manipulation. This does not mean, though, that we have to consider Beckett as an ally. On the contrary—and I don't mean now to impugn Beckett's person or his art—it is false, and a form of ideology that supports the bad reality, to transform the social form of manipulation into the *condition humaine*. Indeed, at earlier stages of capitalism its ideologists also attempted over and over again to erect the objective economic conditions that led to class struggle into general conditions of human existence. I will just give one more example of this. When anything bad is being discussed, I always come back to Nietzsche. Nietzsche, for example, made out that proletarian class consciousness was nothing more than the resentment of slaves. And this ideology, as I know only too well from my youth, prevented many decent intellectuals of that time from joining up with the workers' movement, for their consciousness could not tolerate any resentment or support of resentment in an upstanding, moral person. We therefore have the task of breaking through these kinds of inhibition. We cannot do this simply by showing people abstractly the meaninglessness of manipulation, but we must direct our appeal at those strata, by no means so meagre, who experience emotionally something uneasy, distasteful and restrictive about their manipulated condition. I believe we can already speak of a mass experience of this kind. I do not know how large these sections are. They are however much, much greater than the sections we have so far reached, and so there is a major task of mobilization here.

If discontent flares up, it involves millions of people. I will just consider the Federal Republic of Germany. I still remember very distinctly the time when the movement against rearmament, the 'count me out' movement, undoubtedly reached millions of people, though because it had no internal cohesion it broke up in a short space of time. Then again there was a democratic explosion at the time of the *Spiegel* affair, which was also dispersed. The task of the Marxist movement is to give the explosive power of such opposition movements a permanent dynamic. The central problem, in my opinion, is that as far as I can see, this consolation can only be achieved today in one form, that of a movement. Such a movement need in no way be completely uninfluential. It is of course illusory and absurd to believe that a fourth party can immediately be formed in Germany. But after a certain time, a movement could well have an influence on what deputies people elect, in certain areas. This is already no longer illusory. You should not forget that in America the major parties are often forced to make concessions of this kind in certain situations.

I believe we must put an end, once and for all, to illusions of the kind that we could make a real breakthrough in a short space of time. On the other hand we must not fall into pessimism and believe it is absolutely impossible to exert any influence. It is beyond question that in America there are circles that would like to escalate the Vietnam war to the point of using atomic weapons. If they do not venture to put forward these ideas openly, this is already because there is a movement against this, certainly a completely formless and disconnected one, but one that is present and does exert an influence—a certain influence, we should not be metaphysical and demand a categorical yes or no. The question therefore is to indicate the perspective of struggle against manipulation within a movement which knows that it cannot obtain its ideology from the movement itself, but that consciousness must be brought into the movement from outside. 'From outside' does not mean that one will not connect up with real problems, for such a movement will certainly have a future ahead of it, I believe, not a future that brings results in three months, but in a perspective of decades.

Abendroth: Herr Lukács, I completely agree with you in this overall strategic judgement. In particular with respect to the economic basis of the overall process, i.e. the effective transition of the academic intelligentsia and the upper strata of salaried employees who follow this academic intelligentsia ideologically into a social position which corresponds to that of the working class.

Lukács: Yes.

Abendroth: I have however a criticism to register regarding one other point. The situation that arises from this is, in the two most extreme examples of highly industrialized late-capitalist countries, i.e. the U.S.A. and the Federal Republic of Germany, still more contradictory than you seem to me to accept. On the one hand, by virtue of this transformation, the economic transformation which we have spoken of, with the effect that the interests of the intellectual strata are linked objectively with those of all employed people, we can frequently observe movements which take up the struggle against manipulation at whatever is the dominant strategic point at the given time. On the other hand, however, and moreover more strongly here in the Federal Republic than in the United States, because of the particular German social tradition which we have already spoken of, irrational spontaneous reactions crop up again and again, based on the tradition of these strata. These reactions and their ideological concomitants take the form of a tragic consciousness, for which any opposition appears without prospect. Every time a progressive movement meets with a defeat or falls flat on its face, a whole generation passes from this tragic consciousness to lethargy—generation in the short sense of the term. We can already trace this pattern very clearly in the history of the Federal Republic, quite precisely in the case of the 'count me out' movement against rearmament, and also, if not quite so strongly, in the nuclear disarmament movement. As a result, and from a purely ideological point of view (I do not use this term to mean necessarily false ideology, as the Frankfurt School do), the struggle against those forms of alienation that lead to this tragic consciousness, which unfortunately has a considerable foothold even on ostensibly dialectical tendencies in sociology, is quite central and directly important. We must even struggle against some conclusions of the Frankfurt School which are pessimistic or which lead to inactivity.

Lukács: I agree entirely. I would say that what we have called quite generally the beginnings of a crisis of manipulation obviously take on very different national forms, and this development has a quite specific form in Germany. This is why I have had part of my *Destruction of Reason* published by Fischer, and written this foreword, 'The Mastery of the Past', for the great mass of German intellectuals cannot go forward, not only on the question of manipulation, but in the interpretation of manipulation, so to speak, if they do not succeed in mastering the past, i.e. if the Germans do not see that their development must be considered afresh. I don't want to go back to the Peasant War, as Humboldt said in his time, but I will at least assert in this connection that the path was lost in 1848. As you say, this tragic ideology is not an invention of the Frankfurt School, but originates in a remarkable division of German development which already appeared after 1848. I would like to give a literary example here. It is always said in our literary history, and said correctly, that the problems which Hebbel raises in *Herod and Mariamne,* and in *Gyges and his Ring,* were already the beginnings of the 'Nora problem'. The great difference however is that Hebbel sees this as a general, tragic problem and thereby remains the conservative who turned against the revolution of 1848, while Ibsen's Nora makes a contribution towards the real liberation of women. Cultural criticism of the German past, and of all these questions, also forms part of this complex of problems. I have taken here only a peripheral example, as it were, but this example shows just how, even where German development exhibits quite noble and progressive aspects, it is always adulterated with an official conservatism, with an approval of the defeat of 1848. Today this has to be understood, and in my opinion the radical German intelligentsia is evolving far too mild and limited a criticism of German development. If you compare Jaspers's very useful book with my little essay, you can see many examples of these misunderstandings: Jaspers's entire criticism still bears certain fatal, tragic, conservative aspects.

Abendroth: And nevertheless Jaspers's book . . .

Lukács: . . . very useful, very useful, what I am arguing is that the criticism that we need to make today has to intervene even where we regard things as useful, and I would say that this pamphlet should lead us to value Jaspers as an ally.

Abendroth: Undoubtedly . . .

Lukács: Nevertheless the correct tactic is that laid down by Lenin, which I believe we have already spoken of: Lenin considered the Social Revolutionaries as allies as far back as 1905, and yet he continuously criticized their view of society. The movement that we now envisage must have this dialectic to it, and not the sectarian conception in which people must either be 100 per cent in agreement or 100 per cent hostile. The same holds for this inclination to tragedy. I believe something similar is involved when I say that social phenomena are reduced to the *condition humaine.* The movement against manipulation must wage an unyielding struggle against this tendency, which ranges from the ideology that technology is irresistible and atomic war hence unavoidable, through to quite subtle ethical questions. For the time being we have to elaborate a purely theoretical line, but this must enable us to regard anyone committed to this movement as an ally, while simultaneously criticizing these allies in a proper way. In this way we can form a nucleus which can undertake this ideological struggle against manipulation, and is hence also able to reach those strata who are most decisively being denied a real existence today, in very diverse ways, who experience a dull discontent and feel that this manipulated good fortune is no fortune at all.

Abendroth: I completely agree with you, particularly in this last point. Our central task is to develop strategic consciousness from Marxist analysis. In this respect we must firstly accept as allies those forces which dully remonstrate against manipulation, even if they proceed from quite different ideological starting-points, but we must also criticize them, in a completely friendly fashion. A further problem arises in this connection, and in this particular case I am of a different opinion to Lenin. You know Lenin's thesis on the labour aristocracy, in his *Imperialism* for example; he equates the labour aristocracy somewhat uncritically with the better paid sections of the working class, which he sees as the basis for the entry of bourgeois ideology into the workers' movement. Already at that time the reality in the West European countries was somewhat different. If we investigate the German situation of 1914 as a concrete example, to see which sections of the working class began the struggle against the First World War, it was in fact precisely the better paid, more qualified sections of the working class, for the quite simple reason that they were also the most qualified intellectually and were therefore the first to see through the sham of the war of defence, the alleged war of national defence. Here we have then the problem of imbuing the masses with correct consciousness. This requires a nucleus to introduce this consciousness, and such a nucleus, in the concrete situation of the Federal Republic, can certainly not be organized as a party right away. The nucleus must nevertheless be conscious of itself as a unity. Its unity of consciousness will develop out of on-going discussion, and this means a nucleus that works towards getting organized.

Lukács: Does organization not imply something like a party?

Abendroth: Not necessarily. We have certainly not so far discovered the concrete forms, but these are at first, if you like, still the normal ideological forms of permanent discussion.

Lukács: You see, if I can interrupt you at this point, I have often thought that it might be possible to introduce a form of organization taken from a completely reactionary context. The problem is that students who are very radical get lost after they finish their university studies. How would it be if the radical student movement started something analogous to the 'Alte Herren' in the old student corporations, so that at least the elite of those who had been radical students could remain with the movement? This is only, so to speak, a brainwave of mine. I don't attach great importance to it, particularly not to the expression 'Alte Herren', but you see perhaps . . .

Abendroth: We have already attempted this experiment in the Federal Republic. The SDS, as you know, is the broadest movement of the student opposition, though not the only one, and—for all its ultra-radicalism, which unavoidably crops up again and again—it is the most conscious nucleus of the student opposition. In parallel to the SDS we founded a Socialist League for this purpose, with the result that we were all expelled from the Social Democratic Party. But this form also has its limitations, of course, and still does not solve the problem. Put this way, the problem is specific to Germany, but at a deeper level there is more involved than simply a German question; the Federal Republic is only one form of late-capitalist social organization. In other countries solutions of this kind might be quite possible. Indeed groups of different kinds, even proto-parties, have been formed in a whole series of countries, with all the contradictions that necessarily emerge in this connection . . .

Lukács: The problem of the party is quite different in Italy or France from that in Germany, England or the U.S.A.

Abendroth: This is the correct way to see the problem. Polycentrism is the wrong word, in fact a contradiction in terms, but the concrete forms must be based in the specific national conditions. One should never forget . . .

Lukács: I believe we have come onto a very important subject now. To return to my Hegelian hobby-horse of identity, there is on the one hand a world problem of manipulation, and its most general features are common to all countries.

Abendroth: But the truth is concrete.

Lukács: But in every particular country quite new problems arise. If I take the United States, then the illusion of 1945 of a pan-American triumph of the 'American way of life' has been completely shattered, and with it the whole policy of 'roll back', so that in America today, for all its economic, political and military power, the entire set of ideas associated with the 1945 victory is no longer effective and we have to deal with a quite new situation. What certain American journalists, certain senators such as Mansfield, Fulbright, etc. are expressing, is nothing other than the breaking of a deep crisis, which on the one hand is at bottom the crisis of manipulation, but on the other hand has its specific American form. I will not now go into details. The present-day English forms have their specific origins, the French too, and so on.

Abendroth: Yes, my opinion is exactly the same. One must see the differences, but also the connections. One more word, perhaps, on the general problem. You mentioned quite correctly how the international workers' movement had the good fortune to have first a Marx and then a Lenin. You thus stressed the role of the individual in history, which should certainly not be underestimated. There is also I believe another point which should not be overlooked in this connection. In both cases the historic process, as it were, selected the individuals *post festum.* Lenin, in the years between *What is to be Done?* and 1917, was, from the standpoint of the international workers' movement, from the level of consciousness of the movement at that time, one among many —a very questionable one among many . . .

Lukács: Obviously. Only there were certain things about Lenin that were not understood at that time, and which it would have been very useful to understand. In particular, I believe, Lenin's tactic of alliance plus criticism would have been extremely useful for the French party at the time of the Dreyfus affair, which gave rise to a false polarization and seriously damaged the striking power of the party.

Abendroth: For years. There is, by the way, a more recent investigation of this now, a dissertation by Czempiel which you would probably find extremely interesting. The same is also true of the German workers' movement and really for the whole international workers' movement. But there is no reason to wax pessimistic because we cannot see, as it were, the Lenin of today. There is, however, one question which you must consider in the strategic balance, the importance of which extends far beyond the Federal Republic. In none of the late-capitalist countries have we solved the problem of the correct means of communication between the old-style workers' and trade-union movements, on the one hand, and on the other, the various anti-manipulation tendencies among the intellectuals, which are growing into a movement, but which have not yet been able to consolidate themselves. This is really the key to the problem. Without this communication with the broad workers' organizations, the intellectuals cannot succeed—they simply have not got the striking power.

Lukács: This is quite true. I would just like to come back to the question of Lenin, in connection with a completely new problem of organization which crops up again and again in present-day capitalism, every time there is a political tendency which does not represent just a particular capitalist pressure group but the overall interest of capital. I have in mind what in the West is described as a 'brains trust'. Someone like Kennedy knew very well that he was not a theorist or a scientist. And contrary to the European and particularly the German tradition, he did not identify the specialist with the bureaucrat. He realized that he could not learn anything essential from this kind of specialist, but that he needed a selection of intellectuals and theorists; whether Kennedy chose correctly or not is quite beside the point. These theorists were to have nothing else to do but apply their knowledge and energy to general problems, so as to provide material for the politician to use in elaborating slogans for the movement. Now I believe that the particular position of Marx and Lenin has led in the socialist countries to a fantastic overvaluing of the theoretical status of the party first secretary. If in our case for example Rákosi took himself for a successor of Lenin, that was even comic in many respects.

Abendroth: But unfortunately also very tragic . . .

Lukács: Yes, but behind this there is an important question of organization, also for the future workers' movement. If we do not reckon on the political leader, even a very important political leader such as Togliatti, being also a great theorist, then we need a new form of organization which we still have to arrive at in the radical movement and in the workers' movement. This is why I use the word 'brains trust', without attaching undue importance to terminology. I simply mean that a new organizational principle has appeared, i.e. a relationship of duality and collaboration between theory and political practice, which are no longer united in one person as they once were, most accidentally. Today, on account of the extreme extension of tasks, this problem can only be solved with such a dual form. I would like to bring in an example here, again the example of Lenin.

At the beginning of the 1920s, Lenin's understanding of the colonial question was adequate enough to orient the propaganda of the communist parties towards the anti-colonial movement. Today, when particular economic and political problems arise in the liberation struggle of a small country, Ghana or Zambia or anywhere else, there is no one, even if he were of the stature of Marx or Lenin, who could master all these questions. You understand, then, why I lay so much emphasis on the brains trust as a form of organization. I would further like to stress that if there is a stratum which is not suitable for this task, it is the bureaucracy of the state and the workers' movement. For these strata are accustomed to manipulation, and so they are for the time being incapable of an unconstrained and scientific consideration of things which do not yet exist. This is of great importance for the intellectual side of that movement which we both hope to see. This intellectual movement can on the one hand be the vehicle for introducing the new revolutionary consciousness into the workers' movement, while on the other hand it can build up a broad staff for a brains trust. The brains trust of today can perhaps simply consist in someone writing a good book on Egypt or Syria, which exerts an influence on the French or English party's handling of the colonial question in a roundabout way. I am not sure whether you see what I mean here, how this is a quite major task for the intellectuals of today. If our movement begins to understand, for example, that a correct polemic against the manipulating theory of knowledge of neo-positivism can have great political implications in twenty years' time, we can lead a section of intellectuals, the best section, out of this wretched academicism. I have in mind that academicism which you spoke of earlier, and you are completely right that the Frankfurt School also produces a kind of interesting academicism, if I may say so, a secessionist academicism.

Abendroth: I do not want to be misunderstood. I believe that the Frankfurt School, for all its contradictory character, is very useful for the young West German intellectuals.

Lukács: It is contradictory in the sense that there is sómething to be learned from it, but if one wants to learn this, one must break away from Frankfurt.

Abendroth: Yes. But Frankfurt is very frequently the first port of call. It was so for a whole generation of socialist students, one of the most important . . .

Lukács: Yes, I certainly do not want to deny this, and I can only say personally that I do not at all regret today that I took my first lessons in social science from Simmel and Max Weber and not from Kautsky. I don't know whether one cannot even say today that this was a fortunate circumstance for my own development.

Abendroth: Yes, only we should not forget one thing, that in your case it was the late Kautsky that was at issue. The earlier Kautsky still played a positive role.

Lukács: Yes, of course. I don't want to make my own biography into a law of development—that is very far from my intention. I only wanted to support what you said, that it is quite possible for students to spend their first years with the Frankfurt School, but they must then break with it.

Abendroth: I am completely of your opinion, but the strategic problem remains. Your idea of a brains trust is also in my opinion one of the most important keys towards solving the problem, and among socialist and progressive forces in the Federal Republic we think along exactly the same lines. However, we face a tremendous difficulty that is not present to the same extent in the other Western countries, where there are genuinely functioning workers' movement. I am not just thinking of the Italian Communist Party, or the French—despite certain contradictions of the latter. There are also organizations such as the Peoples' Socialist Party in Denmark. But in Germany the only immediate possibility open to such a brains trust, if it is formed, is to stew in its own juice, and the decisive strategic problem is to bring a spontaneously forming brains trust, as it were, into communication with those workers' organizations that still exist, i.e. the trade unions. However, even this is not enough if it doesn't find a political role.

Lukács: My opinion here is that if such a movement arises in Germany, it must never forget the task of liquidating intellectually the old Germany, one aspect of which is obviously Social Democracy. I believe that while there has been an on-going criticism of Communism in Germany, extraordinarily little has been said on the question of German Social Democracy before 1914 and the processes which made the 1914 fiasco nothing accidental.

Abendroth: There is not so little as you think. For even among the bourgeois intelligentsia a few historians are now beginning to acquire some understanding of this, mainly from the purely positivist study of documents, as it were. There is for example Fritz Fischer's presentation of German imperialist war aims in the First World War, which refers to the failure of the SPD.

Lukács: Yes, this is the first sign. It shows that we are on firm ground here, that there is no question of our having invented some kind of false ideology of the old Social Democracy, but that there is a real movement involved. I believe one should point out—and I always try to do so myself—how clearly Engels saw this situation in 1890 already in his *Critique of the Erfurt Programme*, which he criticized for assuming that the whole beautiful beastliness of the old regime would 'grow over into socialism'.

Engels was already aware of this problem in 1890, and if you are trying to link up with the workers' movement, then it is necessary to make people aware of these problems time and again.

Abendroth: Yes, undoubtedly, but although the general strategic programme can certainly take its bearings from our brains trust idea, it is not thereby solved. For in the background there is still a further and very major obstacle, which if it appears most sharply and in a so to speak exaggerated form in the Federal Republic situation, has a weaker parallel in the remaining European capitalist countries. You have previously and quite correctly referred to anti-communist sentiment, which is certainly in retreat, but is nevertheless still a central determinant of the situation in the Federal Republic. It is really impossible to forget that the negative aspects of the brutal, barbaric and degenerate dictatorship of Stalinism had a strong influence on this situation in the workers' movement of the capitalist countries, most strongly of course in the Federal Republic, through the actual existence, side by side, of the two German states. There is also a material side to this question, which once again affects the broad mass of the working class, and also academic workers. In the conjuncture of reconstruction, workers of all categories in the Federal Republic, however diverse, could obtain a standard of living far in excess of that of their counterparts in the GDR. (This by the way was the result of trade-union pressure, and in no way a voluntary concession of capitalism.) This problem is now less acute, but has still not been overcome, although since the economic upswing of the GDR it is on the ebb. The ideologists of capitalism could thus demonstrate—falsely, but successfully—the alleged superiority of the capitalist economy over the socialist economy, setting aside the concrete historical mediations of this problem. One of our ideological tasks is to struggle against this.

Lukács: Yes, and in this connection I would like to stress again and again the tremendous importance that the genuine liquidation of Stalinism in the socialist countries could have for the movements in the capitalist countries.

What we have had up to now is the beginning of a process, what I might rather clumsily call the revocation of Stalinism in the form of Stalinism. I always say that we are for the time being demolishing Stalinism in a Stalinist way, and a genuine demolition will only succeed when we break radically with Stalinist methods. To take two examples: in 1953 the political police was liquidated in the Soviet Union as a state within the state, and Beria had to be executed for this liquidation to be successful. In 1966 in Yugoslavia Ranković could simply be dismissed and the autonomy of his organization abolished. Only when this beginning is energetically carried through in all socialist states can there be talk of a genuine liquidation of Stalinism in this respect. It is also worthy of attention that in the West also, the secret organization of the political police as a state within the state is not sufficiently considered; it is even glorified in detective films. In the United States, in my opinion, this state within the state is expanding in many respects. I do not believe that it has as yet the power of, let us say, the N.K.V.D. in the 1930s, with the Moscow trials, but certain things in South America, the events in Santo Domingo, etc., are just as independent acts of the secret organizations as the great trials were independent acts of Stalin's secret organization . . .

Abendroth: And in Santo Domingo, with at least as great barbarity, as it were, if on a smaller scale . . .

Lukács: Yes, and I would say in passing that the struggle against manipulation does not only involve the manipulation of consumption, but also this form of political manipulation, so that United States foreign policy, for example, has in many respects ceased to be democratically conducted, despite its ostensibly democratic character. This is quite clearly observable in Kennedy's actions in connection with Cuba. Kennedy waged a continuous struggle against the illegal intervention of the secret organizations, while today under the Johnson regime this intervention of the secret organizations and the military bureaucracy is incomparably greater. You can see here how manipulation similarly involves major political phenomena. And here I believe it is the duty of Western intellectuals not simply to follow the tradition of Koestler and struggle against the Soviet N.K.V.D., making this into a kind of ritual, but rather to show that the same kind of thing exists in other forms in other countries. If this system has so far not developed to such a power in the Federal Republic, this is partly the effect of certain explosions of public opinion. I believe that, if public opinion had not exploded at the time of the *Spiegel* affair and had not led to the fall of Strauss, we would already have a moderate kind of McCarthy system in politics there.

Abendroth: I don't think it would have been all that moderate . . .

Lukács: I think you understand what I am getting at, that it is important to indicate certain common features of the systems of manipulation and their dangerous consequences. This would lead us to certain conclusions which also concern life in the Federal Republic in general. I have in mind for example a question which I know only from particular cases and cannot form a general judgement on. In judicial practice in the Federal Republic, a judge's verdict and an expert's report are made into fetishes, which makes a revision of obviously false verdicts very much more difficult. I think you are quite familiar with this, certainly far more than I am; I have the feeling that these things have to be struggled against, whereas essentially only *Der Spiegel* is waging such a struggle in Germany today, only in particular cases and not always with the necessary consistency. We are considering something which affects the lives of very many people. Here you have a question of manipulation which can very well be used to arouse mass movements.

It is no accident that obvious miscarriages of justice have aroused mass movements in bourgeois society in earlier times, the Dreyfus case being the greatest of these. One example of the effectiveness of this in literature is Arnold Zweig's novel about Sergeant Grischa, which, all things considered, is very good and useful, and exposes certain aspects of the German state apparatus in connection with a court verdict. I believe that the sham democratic side of the Federal Republic could be revealed more clearly by a good analysis of certain specific verdicts, rejections of appeals, etc., than by many political questions, and I have the feeling that in this respect many more bad things happen in the Federal Republic than appear in the press and are noticed by public opinion. I don't know what you would say to this . . .

Abendroth: I completely agree—of course very many more bad things take place than the public ever learn about. You know, at first this criticism was directed at the practice of political trials, whereas it would seem that one could make the problem more clear to the masses if one dealt with other trials also. This however raises a quite general problem, which I believe is important far outside the borders of the Federal Republic, in fact in all societies of this type. The problem is that the defence against such tendencies starts out from the basis of formal democracy. The task however is to move from the defensive vindication of democratic rights, in the first instance of bourgeois-democratic rights, onto the offensive struggle against manipulation.

Lukács: I am in complete agreement. I would just like to emphasize here this specifically German situation, where an expert appointed by the court represents above all the holy state, and nothing he says can be discussed as a scientific opinion. An authoritative decision thus arises, and anyone who protests against it is automatically a bad citizen. I don't know exactly where—I have a bad memory for names—but there was a trial of this kind somewhere in the Rhineland not long ago, with a person who had most probably just been awkward, who was simply shut up in an asylum for a while because his name had cropped up in a murder case, and where it was subsequently shown that the authorities had been very careless in their investigations. This is, I might say, a phenomenon almost specific to the German public authorities, i.e. that a public prosecutor or a judge who does something wrong represents the holiness of the state, the holiness of the authorities, even in his errors, and there is a certain tendency to gloss over this, to keep it from the public eye. I believe that an anti-manipulation movement in Germany would have a very great field of action in this area, for it is something which everyone is interested in. I don't mean that the individual case is so important, what is important is to unmask the methods of procedure of the judicial apparatus. The field of struggle against manipulation is thus much wider than one might at first sight believe.

Abendroth: I am completely of your opinion; I simply believe that this is not only a special German problem, although there are two reasons why it is more obdurate in the Federal Republic of Germany. On the one hand there is the tradition of governmental ideology, on the other hand the fact that the judicial stratum of the Federal Republic is still identical with that of the Third Reich. But there are problems of a similar kind in all bourgeois societies.

Lukács: I am fully convinced of that. It is still no accident, however, that the greatest scandal of this kind to explode was the Dreyfus case. I am convinced that in Germany at that time there were twenty Dreyfus cases, which however no one made any fuss about. So the Dreyfus case does not only show that there is something general involved here, but the explosion it created clearly brings out the distinction between Germany and France.

Abendroth: If you take the United States for example, they have quite similar situations there, certainly more directly political great trials and the like, and also without anything being generated in the way of counter-movements.

Lukács: Yes, of course, I would not contest that at all. I only mean that we should not confine the struggle against manipulation to problems of free time in the narrower sense and manipulations of an economic kind, but should rather see that this technique of manipulation, which is partly an inheritance of earlier times, which has simply been remodelled, penetrates the whole of everyone's life, and that we can therefore count on certain feelings of discontent or discomfort among far wider strata, that we have thus a direct way of reaching these strata.

Abendroth: Indeed, but the same basic problem remains—and

I am glad that we can maintain the same view here—that the struggle against the late-capitalist social structure involves the defence and extension of the rights of the individual, such as democratic rights and the right of participation. And here a general question emerges, the consideration that, although the ostensibly democratic legality of the bourgeois capitalist state is largely the product of manipulation, the establishment and extension of these democratic rights, and the movement forward on this basis, can possibly become, even in the bourgeois state, the direct point for the transformation of bourgeois into socialist society. Bourgeois, capitalist society, even late-capitalist society, certainly concedes rights and seeks to use them to its own advantage, as means of integration, but when certain problems come to a head, it not only neutralizes them manipulatively, but even does away with them in serious cases.

Lukács: Yes, this is a problem which also crops up continually in connection with the liquidation of Stalinism, i.e. the distinction between revolutionary conditions and conditions in a consolidated society. There is no question but that, as regards a revolutionary situation, the remark that Lenin once directed at Gorky is quite apposite. When Gorky complained that an injustice had been committed somewhere in the provinces, Lenin said to him with a laugh, 'Yes, if people are brawling in a pub, how will they establish which blows are necessary and which are no longer necessary?' This sounds a little cynical, but I don't think that Lenin meant it at all cynically. When it is a question of life and death, of existence and non-existence, then certain things which in normal circumstances are absolutely necessary —the legal form of which is the English Habeas Corpus Act— will be consciously set aside by a class that is struggling for its existence. It was something quite different, however, when Stalin extended this setting aside in periods when it was absolutely superfluous. The Trotskyists and Bukharinists were already completely defeated politically by the time of the great trials, and Talleyrand's *bon mot*, '*C'est plus qu'un crime, c'est une faute*', is equally applicable here. At present we are in a relatively consolidated situation, and so what you say is completely true. It must be understood, however, that when it is a matter of life and death, the position is quite different. At the present time this task of an anti-manipulation movement must be particularly stressed, especially since the bourgeoisie, the German bourgeoisie in particular, but also the American, has a great tendency to transform situations in which it is not at all endangered into periods of oppression with the slogan, 'The country is in danger.' I spoke earlier about judicial practice, and it is also significant in this connection that the point there is not to establish the real facts of a case but rather to confirm the authority of the court. Here again problems arise which we can only bring to people's attention by a concrete historical treatment . . .

Abendroth: . . . this is why the struggle for the defence of the constitution against the emergency laws is of pressing importance today in the Federal Republic of Germany, though there are parallel problems in a whole series of other states. On this issue we were able to establish a broad united front.

Lukács: This emergency legislation is really nothing more than the legal preparation for the total abolition of democratic rights and freedoms, which the bourgeoisie is already abusing. Indeed, you should certainly not forget that Bismarck already very cleverly took over certain democratic forms from the West—this is an important feature of German development.

Abendroth: Universal suffrage for the North German Reichstag in 1867 . . .

Lukács: . . . universal suffrage—at the same time, however, he made sure that these forms would remain completely ineffective in Germany. We always come back to this fundamental point, that the question is to struggle for a *de facto* democracy, not a paper democracy. Today, one could say, paper democracy reigns the world over; even in Stalin's time the secret ballot, and anything you like, was guaranteed on paper. The real slogan today must be to transform the paper democracy, which is present everywhere, into a *de facto* democracy, for this is the point at which things really come to a head.

Abendroth: Exactly! And here we in Germany will shortly have to link our struggle against the emergency laws with the trade-union struggle for co-determination, with the extension of industrial democracy. The two things are of course objectively related, and it is our task to provide a common denominator for them. This is precisely the way to form the consolidating nucleus which will enable the relatively popular issue of defence of the constitution to be linked to the general problem of the democratization of society and hence to the transition to socialism.

Lukács: Yes, you see, once again the thing is like this: a *de facto* democracy can only be defended in particular cases. Everyone will agree with the general slogan of a *de facto* democracy; from Adenauer to Wehner there is no one who would say, 'I want to do away with *de facto* democracy'. They will even say that the emergency laws are designed to secure *de facto* democracy. Thus it is not a question of general slogans, but of demonstrating this contradiction in every person's life.

Abendroth: Here however we come up against another side of the problem. This struggle for the transformation of paper democracy, the appearance of democracy which is all that bourgeois society guarantees, into a genuine democracy, which would put life into the democratic rights of the broad masses and also emancipate them culturally, making them capable of self-government, is in reality nothing else than the struggle for the transformation of late-capitalist social forms into socialist relations.

Lukács: Obviously, and here indeed lies an interesting problem, which social science can do very much to enlighten us about. For in my opinion it was the great French Revolution that introduced an opposition between liberal capitalist and democratic society, which was previously only suspected. It seemed at the beginning of the nineteenth century that the bourgeoisie's ideal of liberal capitalism was being threatened to an increasing extent by democracy. Hence the spread of pessimism, which you can study very well in such important theorists as de Tocqueville and J. S. Mill. On the other hand there appeared the Russian democratic critics—Belinski, Chernyshevsky and Dobroliubov. Their international significance, in my opinion, is that they represented, very decisively, the other side of this opposition.

Today this struggle has in a certain sense been neutralized. Social democracy, which regarded genuine democracy as the precondition for socialism, has been most unsuccessful in practice. In this connection I believe that the positive side of Jaurès's work is greatly undervalued today. Bourgeois ideology has been able to reconcile liberalism and democracy on the basis of the technical manipulation which modern sociology has provided, but this reconciliation breaks down the moment that democracy ceases to mean manipulated democracy. I believe that a just and correct historical presentation of this question in relation to the class struggles of the nineteenth century could again be very helpful in convincing certain intellectual strata. We must put an end to the contempt for the nineteenth century that was very fashionable for a long time. Marx himself certainly belongs to the nineteenth century, and without a history of the nineteenth century we will not be able to put our aspirations on a firm footing. If we said that manipulation had arisen as a result of technical development, then we would have to be machine-wreckers, against technical development, to struggle against this manipulation. If we see that the rise of manipulation is only the culmination of a major development at the general social level, which grew out of the contradictions of the great French Revolution, then we obtain a quite different purchase on this question. Such a treatment of the history of social movements and of the social sciences would be a very important task.

Abendroth: Yes. It is no accident that neo-positivist tendencies in sociology, and also their counterparts in the mathematical models of economics, have been used to de-historicize problems and hence conceal them.

Lukács: Obviously!

Abendroth: This is the methodological side of the matter, and I completely agree with you that this is one of our central duties as scientists and moreover in our task of introducing the results of scientific work into society. But the matter also has a political side, which is currently important. Owing to the barbaric backwardness of Russian society before the great October revolution, it was no accident that the Russian revolution passed through a stage of high Stalinism; although this was by no means unavoidable, it was nevertheless conditioned by objective circumstances. It was conditioned by such things as the need to solve the problem of primitive accumulation, to abolish illiteracy and enforce industrial discipline in the absence of capitalism.

Lukács: I grant what you say in essentials. However, the theoretical deformation we have spoken of has arisen independently of this, even though the liquidation of Stalinism will help the European and American movements somewhat. It is therefore the duty of Western Marxist movements to put these facts into the correct theoretical and historical perspective; for there are previous occasions when quite small things enabled problems to be completely distorted. Allow me to take a small example from Marx's own work. Marx criticized James Mill for taking the sale of a commodity as the elementary process of capitalism, so to speak; if the formula C-M is taken in isolation, then Mill's analysis would be correct—since every sale is a purchase, and every purchase a sale, there must consequently be a necessary harmony between purchases and sales. In his criticism of Mill Marx situated the isolated formula C-M as one side of the general process of circulation C-M-C, from which the unpleasant fact emerges that, if someone has received money in exchange for a commodity, it does not necessarily follow that he is forced to buy another commodity. C-M produces an identity, C-M-C a dialectical result. I have brought this in purely as a methodological example. I am convinced that if you undertook a real analysis of contemporary economic, sociological and other 'universally accepted' truths, you would arrive at a whole series of things to which, *mutatis mutandis,* this scheme could be applied.

A movement such as we both hope to see has a tremendous theoretical task to provide a foundation for its practical work. Just consider how Stalinism turned the conception of partisanship into a caricature. With Lenin the ontologically necessary unification of the theoretical mastery of reality with practice was a step forward not only in human responsibility but also in the objectivity of human knowledge, whereas Stalinism replaced this by the bureaucratic manipulation of all statements. No wonder that the belief of people discontented with capitalism in the ability of Marxist theory or socialist practice to lead them in a new direction has suffered deep shocks. Trust can only be restored by a radical and universal, theoretical as well as practical reckoning with all Stalinist methods. I am not contradicting what I said earlier, that we have to call on people to do away with manipulation, but this appeal will only be effective if we are in a position to show theoretically that what is involved here is not a pre-ordained economic or economico-technical process, but one which is manipulated by a certain class in a certain way. The manipulation of certain axioms, which on closer consideration are not at all valid, is a case in point. That is why I brought in the case of James Mill, where this manipulation is present in a very easily intelligible form. I am convinced that our economics and sociology is full of cases like this and that theoretical criticism and historical analysis can be of extremely great service here.

Abendroth: We must start this off with quite concrete problems such as that of democracy. We should recognize the importance of theoretical analysis, for example, in dealing with the ideology of totalitarianism, which was developed by the ruling class in the West without any attention to the historical background, and in its own class interest simply identified Stalinism and fascism. But here another problem presents itself, that the theory which we formulate and which we precisely have to analyse scientifically and historically, will become a force which grips the masses if it corresponds to a practical need of theirs and also to their practical perspicacity. Right here is one aspect of the problem of democracy. It should be of the greatest help to us in our present struggle to find the formula which could be translated into practical action.

Lukács: I agree with you, I would just like to indicate a certain structural relationship between theory and practice. If we simply dream of finding the special case which will directly stir the masses, then we shall never find it. If however we set in motion a process of comprehensive scientific research and find thirty, forty or fifty such issues, then among the fifty there will be one which can be used to approach the masses. It is in my opinion completely illusory to believe that we can hit on the issue which will transform the discontent of the masses into practice, just by investigation of the economy. We must evolve a broad scientific development, and then, whether he arises from our own ranks, or not, a political leader will emerge who recognizes that criticism no. 37 can be used to move the masses, and who is also in a position to derive a practical political line from it. The stirring slogan must grow out of a collaboration between science and life—i.e. the economic process; you should not forget that none of the slogans with which Lenin overthrew Russian capitalism was a socialist slogan. Immediate end to the war was not a socialist slogan, nor was the division of the land and soil. But Lenin had to be an extremely far-sighted theorist to extract these aspects from the criticism of a semi-feudal capitalist society.

Theory is also very extravagant, since it must encompass very many things, while history shows time and again that any part of theoretical work may relate to the point where the thing explodes. It is very interesting how such a purely scientific theory as that of Galileo, or a few centuries later that of Darwin, led to a—how should I put it—a 'semi-political' explosion. I mean by this that extremely broad and deep theoretical work is a precondition for practice that can in no way be circumvented. None of us, in considering these problems, can know exactly what slogans it will be that bring the resistance to manipulation to an explosion. Since we can only guess approximately, we must attempt to bring the results of our research to the masses. Which slogans will then sink in, we can in no way determine in advance.

Abendroth: I am fully of the same opinion, but there is a very great difficulty in this complex of problems. In the socialist countries, despite the phase of Stalinist degeneration, there is the social basis for broad intellectual work, even if this is still deformed. But precisely in the socialist countries, the *intellectual* basis of a solution to these problems is lacking, both on account of the Stalinist residue and on account of a limitation to their own problems. In the capitalist countries, the reverse is the case, and once again this is most strongly so in the Federal Republic of Germany. The *social* support for critical intellectual activity, purely theoretical activity, is extremely slender and can only be obtained by accident. In the Federal Republic this is still worse than in the United States.

Lukács: I accept this completely, only do not forget that this situation is in a certain sense characteristic of any capitalist society. Take Balzac's portrayal of the France of his time in *Lost Illusions;* the small group around the figure of Balzac was then itself small, lonely and isolated, and the corruption which Balzac excellently described was there a matter of the press and literature. There was also a kind of manipulation, on the basis of the capitalism of that time, of course in a different fashion to that today. Think of the three different reviews which Lucien du Rubempré had to write of the same novel in different papers . . .

Abendroth: I know many examples of this from the situation in the Federal Republic . . .

Lukács: Of course . . . what I mean is, you should not forget that manipulative capitalism is a particular new form of capitalism, but a form of capitalism nonetheless. To imagine that we find ourselves in a quite new situation, and to present the nineteenth century as an idyllic realm of freedom or I don't know what, is naturally nonsense. You must not take me for a scientific dogmatist if I believe that the extension of scientific research is a necessary precondition of anti-capitalist development. In Germany one should work to publicize the results which have been reached in other countries—in part this is indeed already happening. I have in mind, for example, the extremely interesting investigations of the unfortunately now deceased C. Wright

Mills, who in places has provided an excellent criticism of American manipulation.

Abendroth: It is also enormously interesting with respect to C. Wright Mills that he began his critical work with a knowledge of Weber, but not of Marx, and was finally thrust up against the real problem through the results of his own activity.

Lukács: Yes, there seems to be a growing interest in Marxism in America, in the United States, developing in a spontaneous way. And there once again it is very important for these movements, which are very weak in every country, to establish an international connection. One should therefore translate into German the best works produced anywhere in the world, whether in capitalist or in socialist countries. If I spoke earlier of a brains trust, what I really meant was the indispensible precondition for the movement to be supported on all fronts by a science which aims at discovering reality such as it is. Without basing itself on a new science and without a criticism of the old science, from philosophy through to all other disciplines, the movement cannot break out of its present isolation.

Adendroth: I am completely of your opinion, only we should see the difficulties involved. The necessity of internationalizing, so to speak, intellectual contact between all the beginnings made in this direction is so much the greater, in that we are confronted by much greater difficulties than were the circles of intellectuals who, as followers of Marx and Engels, joined the growing workers' movement at the time of the First and the beginning of the Second Internationals. Today we are faced with very, very complicated problems, and we have to master much more material than was necessary at that time.

Lukács: This is all correct, but I would not compare the historical situation today with that of Marx and Engels. You should not forget that there were already great strikes in France, and the beginnings of the Chartist movement in England, when Marx and Engels appeared. We must essentially compare our situation with that in which people like Fourier or Sismondi found themselves at the beginning of the nineteenth century.

We can only really act if we understand that this is the situation in which we find ourselves and that the road from Fourier to Marx, both in theory and in its practical elaboration, is in a certain sense still a task of the future. I think you understand what I mean by this.

In the *Eighteenth Brumaire* Marx contrasted the brilliance of bourgeois revolutions with proletarian revolutions, and said something to the effect that self-criticism was the essence of proletarian revolutions, that proletarian revolutions return to their earlier stages with a fierce self-criticism and attack the errors of their first attempts. I believe it is again very interesting that Stalinism promoted a tremendous display of self-criticism, while in its theory of self-criticism precisely what Marx said about self-criticism was completely lacking and had to be lacking. I believe you understand what I am driving at, that we must reach an understanding free of illusions as to where we stand today, in order really to accomplish that which today is really there to be accomplished. And today—I would underline the word 'today' —the possible future importance of theoretical results which can not yet be brought to the masses at all, should not be underestimated.

I believe it is no contradiction to say that a movement against manipulation, a movement for genuine democracy, can condemn itself to inactivity by excessive practicalism. The potential effect of theoretical discoveries cannot be valued highly enough in this connection. We have already spoken earlier, for example, of the influence that religious movements have even today. Theoretical clarification, genuinely philosophical theoretical clarification, is absolutely necessary here; the phenomena of the present crisis cannot simply be taken theoretically at face value. I refer here again to the case of Garaudy and Teilhard de Chardin. This gives rise to an illusory way of thinking which leads nowhere, while it is completely possible by means of correct criticism, by a genuine philosophical analysis of what is happening in the Protestant church, for example, by way of de-mythologization, to have a great effect firstly on a few people, then on whole strata. We have the task today of preparing such a movement. Don't misunderstand me, we must of course seize every opportunity, but on the other hand we must also not underestimate the importance for this movement of purely theoretical research, and not fall into the error of holding this to be a *quantité négligeable*. Obviously not every socialist worker in Germany has read all of Marx and understood the whole theory of surplus value, but I believe that the movements in Germany, France and Italy would never have arisen without *Capital*, that very complex relationships are involved, and that theoretical foundations will also play a tremendous role for that movement which you and I are both, I would say, dreaming of.

Abendroth: I am particularly grateful for the last conclusion that you have drawn. It still comes down, however, to translating the mere dream into reality.

Lukács: Of course, of course . . .

Abendroth: This demands a tremendous intellectual work, but an intellectual work continuing on the basis laid by Marx, Engels and Lenin. We must create a historical consciousness of the proper identity in non-identity.

Lukács: And we must arouse a historical consciousness both in the intellectuals and in the broad masses—which is of course a very difficult thing to do—for manipulation leads, again and again, as you described very correctly in connection with the tragic consciousness and similar phenomena, to seeing *conditions* as a final ontological form of existence, while the real ontological form of existence is the *process*. If you study the analysis of essence and appearance in Marx, then the appearance is always related to the essence in such a way that the process has vanished from it. Marx shows repeatedly in the case of money and other questions, that people can manipulate these things quite well (in the contemporary expression), although they have transformed the real process into a condition of reification. One great task which we must strive to accomplish is to demonstrate, at first in the area of theory, that all these conditions and reifications are only forms of appearance of real processes. In this way we will gradually make people understand that they should experience their own lives also as a historical process. This is tremendously important, but I believe it is not impossible as a future perspective.

Fourth Conversation

Georg Lukács—Wolfgang Abendroth—Hans Heinz Holz

Provisional Summary

Holz: Herr Lukács, over the past few days we have discussed from different angles various problems relating to the basis of your philosophical conceptions, from the general foundation of an ontology of social being up to topical questions of practical historical action in present political conditions.

In this process we have covered many fundamental questions, and if we are together today for the last time, it only remains perhaps for us to settle a few points which have already been touched on on previous days, but not yet completely developed. The question which has been particularly important for me in our conversations and which I have become aware of as a problem, is how a Marxist view of history, which deals with objective necessities, should regard the problem of subjective freedom, i.e. the problematic of possibility, of the objective space of possibility within the social object. I believe that what you have said on this question provides certain definite perspectives and guidelines.

Lukács: Yes, I believe that in this respect also, the correct interpretation of Marx must be an ontological one. The major difficulty of this is that Marxism on the one hand describes certain basic features of the historical process, which it says operate in a certain sense independently of what men in their actions desire and intend. On the other hand it is also of the essence of Marxism that the decisions that classes, peoples, and in certain circumstances even individual men make among alternatives, play a definite role in history. This can give rise on the one hand to a kind of voluntarism, from anarchistic voluntarism to the bureaucratic voluntarism that prevailed in the Stalin era, on the other hand to a mechanical, mechanistic cult of necessity which was for example widespread in the Second International. In the theorists of this period, Plekhanov for example, we find a kind of duality, necessity in economics and a kind of optionality in the realm of ideology. I believe, however, that a dual movement can be observed within the economy itself. I think you will certainly have understood from my earlier presentation that the economy is also made up of the teleological projects of individuals. From an ontological point of view, every economic act involves a choice among alternatives, for example technological decisions in the production process, or whether a certain person buys this or that commodity. This space for decision permeates the entire economy. Now I believe I can establish, from studying the question itself and also from the study of Marx, that there are in the economy what one might call three major dynamic factors, which have developed uninterruptedly in the course of human development, independent of what the bearers of their development desired. They seem at first sight to be very simple and elementary.

The first factor is that the quantity of labour which is necessary for the physical reproduction of a human being tends constantly to decrease. In the case of primitive man, his entire life was occupied with his own physical reproduction. Today, on the other hand, the reproduction of mere physical existence is a minimal part of the labour performed by a society. In studying history, you come across certain very important turning-points in this process. For example the rise of slavery, in place of simply killing prisoners of war or even of cannibalism, began when the slave was in a position to produce more than was needed for his own reproduction. Before this it would have been completely senseless to keep slaves, and so of course no slaves were kept. I believe there is an uninterrupted dynamic development in this direction from the Old Stone Age through to today. Let us leave aside whether or not this process takes place in a straight line. This is in my opinion one factor of historical determinacy.

The second factor is that labour was of course originally

dominated by natural conditions. In the primitive Old Stone Age, for example, stones, just as they were found, were the starting-point of labour. From that point on, however, a development took place in which labour, the division of labour resulting from it, and everything which was erected on this basis, became ever more socialized. In other words, social categories form an ever more cohesive layer, which is erected over the physiologically given human existence and even modifies this. You will recall that Marx once said very nicely that hunger is hunger, but that the hunger which is satisfied with cooked meat, knife and fork is something quite different from that satisfied simply by tearing at raw flesh. And it is precisely with the satisfaction of the deepest physiological needs, i.e. eating and sexuality, that one can best study how human functions become ever more strongly socialized —in a definite sense of this term. Marx calls this a retreat of the natural boundary. The word 'retreat' is necessary here, for the natural boundary will never completely disappear, by virtue of the fact that man is a physiologically determined living species. But no one who considers for example the development from foot travel to the plane travel of today, will deny that such a development is taking place. Here again, therefore, we have quite clearly a process in human development that is independent of men's will. For there were very important periods in which many people, such as the ruling classes, wanted to hold back this development, as in late Athens, in certain periods of the Middle Ages, in the Restoration era after the French Revolution, etc. But it is important precisely in this connection to show that it is impossible to hold back this development, that there is an un-interrupted development in this real socialization of human society, as one might call it, though indeed things are not quite the same in the ideological problems of the superstructure.

The third factor, which is very closely related to the other two, is the ever stronger integration between different societies. I believe that the original human tribes were very small and could even not have existed otherwise. From then on, through Greece, Rome, the Middle Ages and so on a development has taken place which has created, in the world market, the economic basis of human unification. Consider for example, how—to take the era of classical antiquity—while there was a great Mediterranean culture from the Hellenistic east across to Rome, there was at the same time a very important culture in China. These two, however, one could almost say, had nothing at all to do with one another, whereas today nothing can happen in the most remote corner of Africa which does not exert a certain influence on the life of, for example, a German worker, even if not a directly traceable one. This process of integration proceeds by necessity, and precisely here you can see that human reactions to it are in no way a direct consequence of the conscious behaviour of these men. There is no question of men having in any way consciously desired this development; the relative and only incipient unity of Greece, for example, was expressed in bitter struggles between the individual city states. And it is well known how later integrations—for example those which led to the modern nations, which were fought for in a bitter struggle against feudalism and feudal particularism—developed self-awareness only relatively lately. It is still a weakness of Germany today that this struggle was not carried out with the same energy as in France or England. And if you see a global unity today, it consists of a sum of revolutions and counter-revolutions, it consists for example in the revolt of whites against blacks and blacks against whites in the U.S.A., and it should not be forgotten here that in a less integrated era, when slavery reigned unchallenged in the South of the United States, these antagonisms were for a long while not so sharp as they are today. But although antagonisms sharpen, they are reflected in the irresistible process of integration itself. I stress with all these things that there is no question of their production by a unified human activity, of which men are already fully conscious, that men desire a unified mankind somewhat as, for example, certain tendencies among the Roman Stoics wanted this. There is rather an uninterrupted process of integration, which naturally also has its ideological representatives. But it is a question of a process which is always accomplished in the form of sharp antagonisms—which become even sharper in the course of integration—even against the will of men.

I believe that these three great processes can be established as objective economic tendencies, and that they should be considered as necessary ones. Insofar as these are economic necessities, we come to establish them in the course of historical development—I don't want to derive them by logic or in that kind of way. Now there is a dialectical relationship between this essence of the economic development and the corresponding realm of appearance—I use the term 'realm of appearance' in the Hegelian sense, in which appearance is also conceived as reality, and not for example in the Kantian sense, according to which appearance would be something produced by man in opposition to the thing-in-itself. In this realm of appearance there is a permanent fluctuation and reciprocal interaction, for in speaking of the essence, I disregarded the most diverse forms in which the thing appears, and the appearance can vary very greatly even within the same process. Just consider, to take something simple, the contrast between Athens and Sparta in antiquity, think of the contrast between the development of capitalism in England and in France. In the development of capitalism, for example, it is clear that economically, it is a case of the same development. Despite this—and I would like to stress here that we are only dealing with the area of economics—English capitalism completely destroyed the smallholding property of the yeomanry, who fought for the English revolution, a century later, while the French Revolution established a smallholding peasantry, which essentially exists to this day. So I believe that the law of the irresistibility of capitalist development gave rise to completely different forms in two such important capitalist countries as England and France, just at the economic level—I would like to underline the word 'economic'—not to speak of ideological forms.

Holz: But these different forms of appearance are nevertheless still founded primarily in necessity.

Lukács: They are both founded in the same essential development, but this essential development takes place in history concretely and uniquely, and can therefore assume very different physiognomies even in the same era and at the same stage of development. I believe we must differentiate ontologically within the economy between the lawbound essential part and the realm of appearance. Hegel said very neatly that essence is a latent form of appearance. I would interpret the latent form epistemologically, so that there is concealed in it, very much concealed, something like Aristotle's unmoved mover. If we wanted to express this in the radically new terminology of ontology, we would have to say that what is involved here is the rectilinear and irresistible character of the process, as opposed to the variegated diversity of its forms of appearance.

Holz: Contingency also emerges within the forms of appearance.

Lukács: Yes, of course, and here, as I see it, there emerge complicated interactions with nature, in which the social and economic factor is of course again the dominant; for whether a natural force, a natural element, promotes or inhibits the economic development is decided by the economy itself. Whether or not coal has a central importance for the wealth of a country depends on production and not on coal. It is not the coal which determines that a country is rich or poor, but rather the stage of socio-economic development in which the country finds itself which determines whether coal is important. We can see this today, when coal is going out of fashion.

Holz: Yes . . .

Lukács: After coal has been dominant for two or three hundred years, coal resources are ceasing to have a positive significance for the economy, and are rather becoming an embarrassment, as you are experiencing now in the Ruhr.

Abendroth: I would like to put in a word, partly by way of objection, partly extension. Natural conditions can have very great importance for productive activity at the beginning of the process of human socialization. But as the natural boundary systematically retreats in the face of human productive labour, so also the economy becomes more independent of simple natural conditions, in this case the existence of workable coal deposits. The presence in nature of any kind of resource, for example coal, could and still can provide the impulse for the development of a particular phenomenal form of this overall developmental process of human socialization through productive labour . . .

Lukács: Of course . . .

Abendroth: . . . while later losing its importance more and more. The predominance of the economy in this process is thus far more restricted at the beginning of the process than at the end.

Lukács: You see, this is possible. It is at all events the case that it was always economic reasons that gave coal this importance. And it is again economic reasons that are pushing it into the background, very economic reasons, so that what is involved is essentially not a technological matter, but rather the greater cheapness of oil. Technologically, all industries could be left to function just as they were with coal, but since oil is so many per cent cheaper—I can't give you the exact figure—coal is being forced out. What is essentially happening is not a battle between certain natural powers; the natural powers are rather chess pieces which the commodity economy moves to and fro, the cheap pushing out the dearer.

Abendroth: Undoubtedly, but there is another factor to be taken into consideration here, that the socialization of the productive process pushes back the natural element as a condition of this process.

Lukács: Only I believe that if one were to analyse these things, for example the transition from the Bronze Age to the Iron Age, one would find in the final analysis the same predominance of the economy as today. Quantitatively, however, the extent of this may constantly increase, and here I am in complete agreement with you. We can observe the same thing in the area of social ideology, that there also the natural boundary is pushed ever further back, and then assumes quite fantastic forms, so that certain philosophers believe that space has got smaller and time faster and so on. That is quite simply nothing else than a purely ideological interpretation of this process. I would like to return now to how this irresistible process takes place in the realm of appearance in these disparate forms, and here, as a result of the principle of socialization, an ever greater superstructure is deposited on top of this economic level. I believe it is very easy to understand how, as long as a small group of men consumed what they themselves produced, ideology could make do with tradition, with the memory of old people, etc. But when trade in commodities appears, as it necessarily does by a simple quantitative increase, at first on the periphery of the small community, later permeating the community itself, this commodity trade necessarily involves a legal system. This is, I believe, only one example of how the increasing complexity of the realm of appearance, which follows necessarily from these three principles, also involves a superstructure, and therefore on top of this latent essence, in the Hegelian sense, which in reality is simply an unequivocal movement of the essence, a very complicated, multilateral and diverse realm of appearance is erected, in which individual teleological projects play an incomparably greater role, though they are certainly not absolutely decisive. It was thus economically absolutely necessary, as a consequence of the development of the productive forces, for slavery to collapse and the feudal labour of serfs to appear in its place. But what forms serfdom assumed in different countries depended on the various forms of activity of the men in question; I don't want to go into the details of this here. We now arrive at the kind of variegation which led Marx to say, very correctly, that men make their own history, but not under circumstances of their own choosing; this fundamental basis, these circumstances not of men's own choosing, includes those economic regularities, this economic essence, which I spoke of earlier. We can thus construct the entire gamut of social development starting from one fixed point, from a characteristic social development which is irresistible. Different peoples can invent the most diverse forms. In South Africa such a thing as apartheid could be conceived. Yet it is quite certain that things are moving towards the integration of the whole of mankind one fine day. What is not at all certain, and now I come to the decisive question, is the form this integration will take. And this leads to the important question, which in my opinion is of decisive importance for the understanding of Marxism—whether we see socialism as a necessary, irresistible product of the essence, or whether we believe that the essential development only produces these basic tendencies which make socialism economically possible. I believe I am interpreting Marx correctly in this respect, for even in his most political texts, in the *Communist Manifesto* for instance, the outcome of class struggles is always conceived in the form of an alternative. Thus I see economic development as creating only the conditions for the victory of socialism. I believe this is not just an accidental aside in the *Communist Manifesto*, and one can see this from what Marx in the *Critique of the Gotha Programme* called one of the pre-conditions of communism, that work must cease to be a compulsion and become life's prime want. The purely objective development of labour certainly reduces necessary labour to an ever smaller minimum, but it would run counter to social ontology to believe that this development could transform labour into a need of life. Men themselves must rather make labour, at a certain stage, into a necessity of life.

Holz: There is also a passage in the third volume of *Capital* . . .

Lukács: Yes, there also . . .

Holz: . . . where the element of compulsion is described as insurmountable even in labour.

Lukács: You see, Marx makes this point still more concretely when he says that socialism has the task of making labour ever more worthy of human beings; but labour does not of itself become worthy of human beings, it must be made so by men.

Abendroth: On the other hand, Marx says quite sagely, and certainly correctly, in the same passage, that the reduction of socially necessary labour time is a pre-condition for this humanization of labour.

Lukács: Of course . . . Yes, but the reduction of labour time is a spontaneous process.

Abendroth: But there are also setbacks, Herr Lukács, there is also the idea in Marx that tendencies can succeed which are opposed to the essential development of the total process, particularly through the false alternative outcome of the class struggle, i.e. through the defeat of the oppressed and progressive class, and so even the constant decrease of socially necessary labour time can be blocked in its development and can fall back several stages.

Lukács: I do not rule this out at all. I believe that this irresistibility is intended to be understood on a very large scale, and I would say again that the more highly social a society is, the stronger is the pressure. You must excuse me, but it is in a good Marxist tradition that, in speaking of the real world, I appeal again and again to Balzac. As a great historian of the Restoration period, Balzac showed precisely how the aristocracy came to be the leading force in public life. He showed at the same time, however, how this aristocracy became completely capitalized, how the typical representatives of the aristocracy at this time were essentially agrarian capitalists, who drew the greatest possible profit from the Restoration. In Balzac the few examples of the *cabinet antique,* such as the old feudal lords who retrogressed or remained unchanged and retained their feudal qualities, are pure Don Quixotes, comic figures in the Restoration era. I wanted to say this to you as an example of the opposition we have been speaking of; the intention was to restore France as it was in 1789, yet the genuine supporters of this tendency came to be comical Don Quixotes. In this respect I find Balzac a quite great historian, who didn't need a single intellectual contact with Marx to see this duality, i.e. how economic development was irresistible even in opposition to the desire, wishes and thought of the men responsible for it. This is precisely what Balzac portrays so splendidly. And I believe that we come across such phenomena time and again in history, although we must naturally always allow for periods of regression of at least a few decades. By simply extracting individual dates, you can of course always arrive at a completely false picture. Here, I believe, we have precisely this characteristic feature of human history, that alternatives are possible within the concrete space of action which the major laws of development prescribe. So it is not as if there could be a kind of freedom in the absolute sense. I believe that absolute freedom is simply an idea of the professors, and freedom in the absolute sense has never existed. Freedom exists rather in the sense that life provides men with concrete alternatives. I believe I already used the expression earlier that man is a responding being, and his freedom consists in his having a choice to make between the possibilities of a particular space of action. What I would add in this connection is that in the complicated continuity of human development man can in certain circumstances choose an alternative which is, so to speak, intrinsically very distant and concealed in the interplay of conditions, and which only much later becomes a genuine, because consciously recognized alternative. I have in mind for example the very interesting positions taken up by the Stoic and Epicurean philosophers in late antiquity, when what they wanted were not real alternatives in the real life of that time, but nevertheless alternatives of human development in general, which makes it clear why much later, up to the French Revolution and beyond, the ideas of the Stoics were still a living force.

Holz: At this point I would like to return to the place which this rise of the alternative assumes in a realist philosophy of history. If I have understood you correctly, then what arises is the objective possibility of an alternative, so that the alternative can become the object of a conscious human decision, if teleological projects are related to the objectively occurring historical process and can hence react on it. Now in the first instance the reaction of a teleological project yet again sets up a new set of objective conditions, and so the sets of conditions become ever more complicated. The result would thus be the growing complexity of the sets of conditions. In other words, a quantitative growth of sets of conditions creates in some place or other a sudden change, which makes a qualitative leap.

Lukács: I would just say here that Engels wrote in a letter that the process of development is certainly a social process, but that it would be a mistake to put no value on the individual phenomenon. I will take, if you once again permit me, a very trivial example. A meeting is called somewhere. The speaker talks. The people in the meeting are opposed to the speaker's proposals, they reject them. But the meeting is peaceful, there is no whistling or booing etc., the people sit quietly. Nevertheless the speaker knows quite well that he has been turned down. I believe I am speaking here of an experience which everyone has participated in, which every concert artist or actor in a theatre can experience daily, that he can tell exactly by the feeling whether his performance has been well or badly received. The great weakness of the mass media is that in their case the audience cannot have such a direct effect. But what I meant to say to you is that this alternative decision by the individual is not a zero quantity. Even when it cannot be expressed in activity, the very complicated development of society depends precisely on the fact that these individual decisions, while they are of course not all-powerful, are neither of no importance, and that it is extremely consequential in society when these individual decisions are integrated into a potentially great historical action and when they are not. For example, at the beginning of the French Revolution the Parisian people were very rebellious, and then one fine day they decided to pull down the Bastille. Now whether the legend of Camille Desmoulins is correct or not, is quite beside the point. There was still the day when these individual decisions were integrated into an act of unprecedented social importance.

Holz: One day men decided . . . that sounds frightfully like existentialism.

Lukács: Yes, you see, I would say that of course existentialism is correct about one thing. I even said in my earlier pamphlet against existentialism that we Marxists have underestimated in a criminal way the importance of individual decisions, despite Engels's warning. I don't know whether you remember that I gave the example there that when the workers of a factory go on strike, 40,000 individual decisions are involved. It is not true that there is just one decision by 40,000 people; the decisions are made by 40,000 individual men, and are then integrated into a decision by the whole factory. Engels is therefore correct when he says that the individual decision cannot simply be put at nothing. It may be such a small quantity that it does not come into practical account, but that does not mean anything ontologically. You understand . . .

Holz: But it is precisely the Sartrean depiction of individual decisions that has most decisively scandalized his Marxist critics, whether Garaudy in France, the Soviet critics, or . . .

Lukács: Yes, you see, I must say that this interests me very little. Obviously people have a tendency to see things in terms of mechanical regularities, whereas the most diverse gradations of necessity are present, up to such considerations as that none of us can determine whether in 1917, if Lenin had not struggled with such energy and obstinacy for the insurrection of 7 November, the insurrection of 7 November would have come about . . .

Abendroth: . . . at least with a victorious outcome . . .

Lukács: . . . and whether two months later an insurrection would have had the same effect. Here again the question is that Russia needed to develop its productive forces beyond the level of 1914. That is an economic fact. But that this assumed a socialist form is the result of human decisions among alternatives. It would of course be very far from my intention to fetishize the importance of this decision of Lenin's. Without the preceding revolutionary movement, without the rise of the Bolshevik party, without the world war, etc., a situation would never have arisen in which a decision such as Lenin's acquired such a decisive power. So I arrive back again at Marx's conception: men make their own history, but not in circumstances of their own choosing. I formulate this now in the thesis that man is a responding being. This means that he only reacts to alternatives that the objective reality puts to him. But he does that by abstracting certain tendencies which are contained in the spontaneous process itself and making these into questions, to which he finds responses. Hence this reaction is no longer a purely spontaneous one. If a lion tears apart an antelope, that is a purely biological process, in which no alternative of any kind is involved. But since man through labour makes his interaction with his environment something questionable, to which a response must be given, this alternative becomes embedded in the historical process.

The metaphysical opposition of freedom and necessity is part of our inheritance from the past, but it should just as little be retained in its inherited form as for example the idea that there can be a teleology independent of causality, that there are on the one hand teleological relationships and on the other hand causal ones. In reality there are causal relationships which are set in motion in a specific way by a teleological initiative, while preserving their causal necessity. Now I believe that, arising from this, the relationship of freedom and necessity is also posed in a new way, in a concrete form, which does not abolish freedom, but rather makes it concrete. I believe we have already spoken of how, if I formulate the concept of freedom purely abstractly, I arrive at the situation of Buridan's ass, which is given a false choice of alternatives, to which no answer is possible. In reality there are never such alternatives, but rather always concrete alternatives of the most diverse kind for concrete decision. Corresponding to this it is only natural that there is a tremendous scale of transition from normal life, where individual decisions are barely more than a zero quantity, to those great historic points at which the position taken by one particular man plays a decisive role.

Here is the reason why social development must be in an insuperable sense uneven. For heterogenous components of one kind or another always come into play in the alternatives and their decision, and on account of their heterogeneity they have an insuperably accidental character. I would like to point out that it was none other than Marx who said that which men a revolutionary movement has as its leaders at a given moment is something insuperably accidental. I believe that Marx would reject any attempt to reduce this accidental element, although it is obviously not at all accidental in the social sense that the French Revolution found so great a stratum of talented and socially unintegrated intellectuals. To that extent this phenomenon is in a certain sense sociologically determined. But attempts to explain concrete personalities such as Danton, Marat, Robespierre, Saint-Just, etc. sociologically on the strength of how this general determination of the real space of action affected them in particular, would of course be nonsensical. Here there is in history an insuperable element of chance, which is just as much a factor of uneven development as the various heterogeneities and discrepancies in the realm of appearance of the economy. These elements of chance and unevenness become all the stronger, the more problems are transformed into ideology. For it would once again be completely false to see ideology in its concrete form as a necessary product of economic development.

There is no doubt that the capitalist economy requires a different juridical regulation than a primitive feudalism needed, for example. However, that this happened in some countries by taking over Roman law, but not in England, just shows that even in such cases the ideological need is not satisfied in absolutely the same way. No one can say that because English capitalism did not take over Roman law, it was not true capitalism and did not function. Here the uneven development is particularly clear. We have two splendid ideological examples of a development from feudal religiosity through the Renaissance to the modern age. Florentine and Venetian painting are both forms of expression of this development, yet both reacted on the development in completely different ways. They belong in a certain sense together, but they belong together as a consequence of their difference. Obviously one can find the most diverse reasons for this. By extending our analysis of the real space of social action which obtained in Venice and in Florence respectively, one can arrive at a definite reference point for this.

Holz: But the landscape conditions in Tuscany naturally also had a different effect on optical sensibility from those of Venice.

Lukács: Yes, I simply believe that this optical effect, which was always present, only became significant for art under certain definite social conditions.

Holz: Naturally.

Lukács: Were the conditions of light in Holland in the thirteenth century not exactly the same as in the time of Rembrandt? It needed the revolution in Holland for these conditions to have the effect that they did on Rembrandt or Vermeer, etc. So I would say here also, that the more society develops, the more clearly the retreating natural boundary is discernible.

Holz: But you can observe the same form of *disegno* in the Etruscans, in the Florentine painting of the Renaissance and, as I see it, still in Magnelli.

Lukács: I would rather not enter into this discussion now. I believe that this thesis, that the object of painting is the same, is far too great an abstraction. Obviously, there is in a certain sense a continuity of human development. And obviously there is a grammar for the synthesis of words into meaningful sentences which is essentially the same for us as it was for Homer. I would not at all contest the fact that there is a constancy in this sense. But what is particularly interesting, what is really worth the trouble to consider, is that within this constancy, each particular case, each artistic phenomenon—to confine ourselves for the moment to art—offers a concrete alternative, although elements of continuity are still present. The most serious problem here is that we have today an unprecedently many-sided and diverse literature, and it is particularly stressed that we are in a 'new era', although the threefold division of lyric, epic and drama has never really been broken down. I know no example of the breakdown of this division. Even the 'modern' writers of today write an anti-novel or an anti-drama, and thus tacitly recognize that there is still a continuing form of drama. Beckett can write an anti-drama, by all means, but in my opinion it is an 'anti' to a development from Sophocles to today, which is not to be confused with the development from Homer to today, for one of Beckett's colleagues will now write an anti-novel. I believe it becomes clear here that the unprecedented flux of social determinations and hence of alternatives is not a river without course or banks, but rather produces very definite determinations and then sticks to them.

I now come to another enduring ontological problem of social development, which is related to this, that society is an extraordinarily complicated complex of complexes, in which there are two opposing poles. On the one hand there is the social totality, which in the final analysis determines the interactions of the individual complexes, and on the other hand there is the complex of the individual person, which forms an indissoluble minimal unity within this process. The process is determined by the interaction of both these poles. This is the process of man's coming-to-be; Engels has described the beginnings of this development very well in terms of labour and the rise of language. The retreat of the natural boundary means, seen from man's point of view, a life that becomes ever more human. A consequence of the unevenness of this development is that the greater humanization of life produces on the other hand ever heightened forms of inhumanity. I have never been able to accept that the dreadful things that fascism for example produced were only a kind of throwback to a primitive period or something like that. Fascism is cruelty and inhumanity in a highly developed capitalist form. A human phenomenon of the type of Eichmann was not possible in the era of cannibalism. I do not believe that this type of person, who made the mass annihilation of human beings into a peaceful bureaucratic occupation, could have developed at that time. This is a product of the imperialist era, and did not exist previously. Even the Inquisition did not know this type of person. It knew only fanatics and politicians.

You understand what I mean by indicating this specificity. Because the process of man's coming-to-be is full of contradictions, the ever greater humanization of man must also produce time and again its opposite extreme, until the process of coming-to-be is completed. In a certain sense, however, it is never completed—hence I believe that Marx was right in letting the economy, the process of man's coming-to-be, remain always a realm of necessity. At this point, however, a complex of problems rears itself, since once men have become Man, the higher ideological forms then develop. The two processes belong together and can only be fully realized in a developed society. Marx pointed out again and again how at earlier stages the process of development can end up in forms that are in a certain sense contradictory to social development, to what at the time is higher social development, what he occasionally called narrow-minded forms, but on the other hand historical anticipations are also possible. I have in mind now Athens, or Florence and Venice, or Holland in the seventeenth century. The problem here is when this process can give rise to something of general social significance. This can only happen with communism. But social development can only create the objective conditions for this communism. Whether these objective conditions lead to a crowning of humanity or a maximum of anti-humanity depends on men themselves. The economic development itself cannot produce it. I believe that in this respect I am correct to apply the alternatives presented in the *Communist Manifesto* to socialism, in so far as I challenge the view that economic development automatically produces socialism. Intelligent people have never imagined that.

Holz: To take up one of Hegel's figures of thought, one could say that the relation of necessity and freedom or of necessity and possibility is precisely the relation of the identity of identity and non-identity.

Lukács: I believe, however, that the moment of freedom assumes ever greater, ever more comprehensive importance, embracing the whole of mankind. As far as the higher ideological forms are concerned, not only art and science, but even in a certain sense ethics, it was formerly believed, time and again, that their significance was confined to a small minority. The earlier moral philosophers were aristocrats, not by birth, but insofar as it was not possible for every man to be a Stoic, to hold a Stoical or Epicurean philosophy. I regard Goethe as a really great ethical figure in this respect, and his importance lies, in my opinion, in his aphorism that the least man may be complete, i.e. that ethical perfection, this completeness, does not depend on intellectual ability, on talent.

Abendroth: But this was not yet practically viable in Goethe's time, for the capitalist era cannot yet give everyone this possibility.

Lukács: No, but Goethe, in my opinion, already puts forward this demand poetically, and the great importance of characters such as Klärchen in *Egmont*, Dorothea in *Hermann and Dorothea*, and Philine in *Wilhelm Meister* is that they show that such a human moral completeness is already possible for quite simple people in quite simple circumstances, even if they have to break with the moral judgements of the generality—as is the case with Philine. I therefore regard Goethe as an exemplary figure in this respect, for it was in his life's work that this general democraticism, which was valid also for the future, was for the first time clearly attained. This was not the case with any single great writer before Goethe or with any ethical system. I believe that Goethe is just as important for the development of this idea as the greatest ethical thinkers of the past. I want to say, therefore, that no matter how much it is the economy that makes all these things possible, they can only be realized through the alternative choices of men.

Abendroth: They can also arise on occasion in the form of mental anticipations, which the economy itself only makes feasible by providing a few elements.

Lukács: Evidently, mental anticipations are extremely common in human history. The continuity of human intellectual development depends precisely on the existence of such anticipations. Every period then makes its selection from the whole of the past according to Molière's principle, '*Je prends mon bien où je le trouve*', and so this continuity is by no means a static immortality. I believe one need only consider the effects of Homer or Shakespeare to understand how these kinds of anticipations can be lost for centuries. Nevertheless mankind does have this objective memory, in a similar sense, as we said earlier, to how there can be a feeling in a meeting hall or theatre even if no one expresses it. I believe that this potential presence of certain tendencies is a most characteristic feature of human development.

Abendroth: That is the key to how any idea is taken up again. This becomes possible through the resumption of a mental anticipation, which is reactivated through a certain parallelism between the objective social problems of an earlier period of social development and questions that have newly arisen. Frequently new answers are even developed under the illusion that the old form of the anticipation, the earlier thought process, is being maintained; the old anticipation is thus repeated with dogmatic fidelity. This is how it was even when Roman law was taken up again.

Lukács: I believe here again that, if man were primarily only a producing and not a responding being, there would be no organ for this continuity. Since life throws up definite real problems, what is particularly needed for the alternatives of the day is selected by individual men and through their action, from this fluidity of ideological continuity.

Holz: It seems to me that we should not leave out a further consideration, which follows precisely from what you have just said. You have spoken of the uneven form of the historical process. But this uneven form leads also to a temporal unevenness, an objective social dissimultaneity. At present, for example, we have the existence side by side of developing and highly developed countries, and even in one country we may have residues of earlier modes of production and earlier social institutions, even though the country is primarily characterized by modern industrial production. Such phenomena, the formally simultaneous existence of different stages of social development which are nevertheless in contact with one another, leads to complicated contradictions in the ideological as well as the real historical process, and therefore increases both the importance of the element of chance and the incalculability of the development.

Lukács: I fully agree with you, but I would protest against the term 'dissimultaneity', for the nature of time is that it passes, and defines that which is present. The most diverse and contrasting social conditions, whether they are found in one country or in the world at large, are interesting precisely because they are simultaneous.

Holz: I don't think that this disproves the importance of the phenomenon.

Lukács: No, I only mean the term. I protest against the term because since Einstein it is very fashionable to use a subjective and subjectively relative notion of time, whereas time is a quite general ontological category, which pays absolutely no heed to the development of human society. We work in time, but ideas such as that time passes more quickly with us, and more slowly in primitive era, etc. are a vulgar Einsteinianism from which Einstein would, I believe, recoil in horror. The whole problem of under-developed cultures depends precisely on this confrontation. As long as there was not yet a world economy, and thus not an effective confrontation, both could peacefully coexist, and there was no problem for the more primitive society. The problem arose when its autochthonous development was interrupted by colonialism. The new problem of confrontation arose simultaneously with the beginning of capitalist development.

Abendroth: That is exactly what is described in the *Communist Manifesto*. This gives us to understand, and indeed strikingly forecasts, how the backward countries which first appear to be transformed into mere passive objects of the capitalist world market dominated by the few industrially developed countries, are at the same time transformed by the process of confrontation itself into subjects of the process. This interaction then immediately assumes most complicated new forms—in our own time.

Lukács: Yes, only again a problem of historical ontology has been raised, one which we in Europe used to pose in a false way. The historical development which we have in Europe, seen from a distance, undoubtedly has a certain rectilinear character—Greece, Rome, Christianity, the Invasions, Feudalism, Capitalism, Socialism, etc.—and it is very easy to project into it a teleological reason, such as Hegel in fact did with his philosophy of history. Now these other developments are very instructive for us, for we can see a differentiation even at the most primitive stage, the rise and dissolution of gentile [clan] society, which already provides certain objective alternatives. So what developed in our case was not a teleological necessity, inherent in the differentiation of labour in gentile society, etc. It was rather that under certain specific circumstances, which science has still to determine more closely, gentile society dissolved in a particular way which led to our specific development. In other circumstances, however, there arose what Marx described as Asiatic relations of production, in which the gentile society does not completely dissolve, but instead becomes the basis of a political superstructure. Marx always based his analysis of this on the fact that this social basis is restored, by itself so to speak, on the occasion of a collapse of the superstructure.

I am speaking only in a quite general sense, just to show that while this development, exhibiting definite tendencies which we can see in our own case in the Mediterranean culture, etc., certainly consists of teleological projects, it does not have as a whole a teleological character. Marx saw it as a great service of Darwin's to have liberated the origin of species from teleology. We must also pay attention to this consideration in the historical process. And here another very interesting category emerges. I believe the non-teleological character of the origin of species can be clearly seen in the observed occurrence of what, from an evolutionary point of view, are blind alleys. I refer for example to insect societies, where many species show a remarkably high level of social development, combined with a fixation to a certain evolutionary stage. To reject the teleological character of a developmental process is to imply that there are tendencies capable of development and tendencies incapable of development, tendencies that reproduce themselves again and again without attaining that dialectical higher development which the Mediterranean cultures for example attained. We must emphasize this great difference between ourselves and the so-called backward peoples, which is in no way to deny that these peoples have at certain times produced very highly developed artistic, philosophical and scientific achievements. This is of the essence of uneven development. The cave paintings of those primitive fishermen and hunters created an art which was only equalled many thousands of years later. Gordon Childe described this very well as a period which must have gone under with a geological shift. Hence the beginning, the new development, was culturally at a much more primitive stage. But since agriculture and stock-rearing appeared in place of fishing and hunting, it stood at a higher level in the objective economic sense. You have there if you like a great example of the way our culture has developed already at this very primitive stage.

Holz: On the other hand, we are now in the position of experiencing these artistic products again as art today, at quite another stage.

Lukács: Of course, this only shows that this uneven development is at the same time a continuous development, the object of which is the coming-to-be of man.

Abendroth: Exactly. On the other hand this refers us once again to the contemporary problem. For since these blind alleys of social development, as we may call them, all the various cultures where the development of the productive forces has stagnated and which are now confronted with industrial capitalist civilization, are human cultures nonetheless, the new phenomenon of the world market, which has been generated by our own development, leads to the integration of mankind and to a new unity. These cultures also have therefore the possibility of a response that would situate them at a new level as subjects in the total process, and draw them—even if changed—into the highest form of global unity produced by the historical process of human development, as members with equal rights.

Lukács: I am in complete agreement with you. Here again we have to see the question in such a way that, in using this category of the blind alley, the difference between a biological blind alley and one of a social kind becomes clear. A biological blind alley is an insurmountable blind alley and cannot be changed in any way, but in human development it is the social that dominates, and hence a blind alley is always only relative. I would say here, if you permit me, that if I imagine Graeco-Roman development without the barbarian invasions, then slavery would have been a blind alley for human development.

Abendroth: Although it is possible that immanent tendencies were already driving beyond slavery; there are many signs of this in late antiquity.

Lukács: I would have thought that the antagonism between the economic position of the colony and the Roman state's centralizing bureaucratic tendencies was insoluble for the Roman state. The invasions and the destruction of the Roman Empire were needed in order to emerge from this blind alley, and so what I describe philosophically as a blind alley is in the social sense something relative. Now I would not say that our contact with those peoples who have remained backward is simply analogous to the barbarian invasions. It is something completely different. Nevertheless it provides the objective possibility for these peoples to emerge, through confrontation with our culture, from what, taken in isolation, is a blind alley.

We now come to the most important question. Marx stressed in the Preface to Volume One of *Capital* that certain developments are necessary, but that one can shorten these developments and lessen the pain they involve by means of scientific knowledge. I regard this thesis of Marx's as extraordinarily important. Marx stresses that scientific knowledge of the process at work is required for this. Now Marx explained capitalist development and gave certain indications of its past and remote past, which was truly a great enough achievement for one man. Marx could not concern himself seriously with Asiatic relations of production. He only touched on this subject most peripherally, though even there he made extraordinarily important discoveries. But as to what relations of production were in Africa, we have no idea at all. We must say quite openly that we are completely ignorant here, and our tendency has been to form highly provisional judgements in thin air on the basis of newspaper articles. I believe this should be said for once with brutal frankness, if we are to manage the honesty that Socrates prescribed and distinguish between what we know and what we do not know. In this case we must put the unknown quite clearly in the foreground. And here again I am forced to direct a major rebuke at Stalinism. In the discussions of the 1920s, I think it was in the trade-union debate, Lenin happened to speak a few words about Chinese conditions and said that he had really no idea of what was happening in South China. Lenin was brutally frank about this, but it did not prevent the Second Congress [of the Comintern] clearly specifying in its theses the tasks of the workers' party in the Chinese revolution. But to discover what was really happening in those countries should have been the duty of Marxist science. It is still not too late for this. But we must stress that the Marxism of the Stalin era did not undertake this work, just as it neglected to publish all Marx's own writings—which would have been child's play—so that we would at least have the whole of Marx in front of us. The Marx-Engels Institute has all these texts, and Riazanov said to me in the 1930s that the manuscript of *Capital* came to around ten thick volumes. It has never been published. We see from the publication of the *Grundrisse* how many new things we have to discover about Marxism. But Stalinism didn't even manage this simple thing. Now this consideration leads to the conclusion that, while Lenin correctly specified the tasks of the workers' parties in the general political sense, and while these movements of colonial liberation have continued to progress, it should have been not only possible for a socialist system, but even its elementary duty, to provide a Marxist history and historical analysis of all these backward peoples. For if we conduct the political struggle without this scientific analysis, then what results from this confrontation will be completely half-baked. Just consider for one moment if *Capital* and Marx's other writings had not existed. Would our working-class politics today not be quite half-baked?

Abendroth: Of course. But I can see still another side to the problem, which should be emphasized. The general premise which we started from leads to the objective possibility of achieving the beginnings of socialist development even under originally unforeseen conditions, and this has been realized in practice, even if at first in a barbaric and distorted form. The Chinese revolution could scarcely be given its strategic recipe either by West European or by Russian Marxism. In these other countries, originally drawn into the capitalist orbit merely as objects, the outlines of a revolutionary theory have been developed, and the elements of Marxism taken up, even if at first in a very half-baked form. But these nationalities must give their response, even if this involves gross contradictions and errors, and must reckon with great sacrifices.

Lukács: Quite right. You see, I agree with this completely, and I would like to introduce a factor which is fundamental to the position we have taken here. It is present already in the theses of the Second World Congress of the Comintern, and is hence quite specific. Colonization was not simply a forcible confrontation of two systems. Both systems rather came into a definite relationship, and indeed this form was already established in the operations of the British East India Company. Capitalism intervened against all reform attempts of the backward peoples, however confused these were to begin with, and based itself on the support of those strata who wanted to maintain the old conditions, in league with the colonizing country. This was the policy that Warren Hastings for example pursued in India. If I consider the contemporary situation and the role of America not only in Vietnam, but also in South America, it is simply the modern continuation of Warren Hastings's policy. This is something which we know exactly, and on which we can take up a precise position, and if European democracy cries 'Down with the traditions of Warren Hastings', then it will have said something scientifically correct and important, even if it is not in the position today to say what should be put in the place of what previously went on in Zambia or Somalia. Here in my opinion is the great omission, and if today there are many young people who are aroused by the situation and are genuinely eager to lend a hand, we must at least put those with scientific talent in a position to help the peoples in question by means of scientific research. I believe that, if the broad stratum of young people in the European countries who are excited today about Vietnam produced between them ten or fifteen good monographs on individual countries, this would be an extremely effective aid for the genuinely progressive forces in those countries.

Abendroth: I completely share your opinion, and in our own institute, for example, the work of Kurst Steinhaus on Vietnam was intended as the first beginning of a little aid. But all this inevitably remains more or less a special case, given the restricted possibilities of Marxist analysis in the West European industrial countries, which can only be produced in accidental, particularly favourable conditions. Since the situation is for the time being the way it is, since on the other hand the still imperialist industrial capitalism of the major countries will inevitably continue for a while to be identified with reactionary ruling strata, the comprador bourgeoisie, etc. in the backward countries and certainly in those societies where the progressive forces, as responding beings, *must* when occasion arises respond to imperialist interventions, even in a half-baked fashion, generally having taken over Marxist knowledge in this half-baked way, it follows that the progressive forces will often make considerable errors, even with inhuman side effects. The difference between Chinese and Indian development since the Second World War, however, shows us that for all these errors, the socialist alternative in these countries nevertheless offers more progressive possibilities than the further toleration of the power position of the old ruling strata and their combination with new capitalist classes which co-operate more or less openly under the leadership of the Western late-capitalist states. The necessary implication of this position seems to me that we must accept, and should not disparage, the errors made by socialist-led revolutions in the developing countries. While we must criticize the inhuman aspects of revolutionary processes of this kind, we should not take this as an occasion for defamation.

Lukács: If you are saying that we should not use errors as a pretext for defamation, I agree with you. On the other hand there are errors which are so evident that they must be unconditionally criticized . . .

Abendroth: Agreed . . .

Lukács: . . . and indeed in the interest of the backward country in question . . .

Abendroth: Of course . . .

Lukács: . . . even if the criticism has, for the moment, no direct effect. I refer once again here to what is in this respect an exemplary policy, how Lenin saw the peasant Social Revolutionary party as a potential ally ever since 1905, but at the same time criticized very sharply and continuously its false ideology. We must break with the false idea which arose in Stalin's popular fronts—i.e. that people who didn't sign declarations were therefore totally reactionary. A popular front, if I dare use this term, which indeed also bears on these problems, is only possible if the conscious elements struggle together according to their capacities at the time, and at the same time criticize each other. I regard the conjunction of these two factors as one of the most important problems of future development. Otherwise we have an unprincipled amalgam, and the worst thing about this is not that non-participants are disparaged, which indeed is bad enough, but that the participants themselves are not criticized. I believe that this is necessary, for if there is a period in which an understanding of these relationships is an unprecedented practical necessity, it is our own, because even in the industrially developed countries the struggle for structural changes requires relations of alliance. This is just as complicated a question as relations with the backward peoples. Here everyone must endeavour to attain maximum clarity, and in my opinion the first condition for this is precisely to distinguish between 'this I know' and 'this I don't know'.

Abendroth: I share your opinion completely, only the starting-point 'this I don't know' is by the nature of things a transient one. It is narrowed down by the concrete experience of each development. Hence the extension of the 'this I know' and consequently of the 'this is concretely what I want today' necessarily puts an end to old alliances of the popular front type as these allies advance, but then inevitably reproduces new questions of 'this I don't know' at a new and higher stage. Just on this account, constant controversy and mutual criticism is indispensable during every popular front, so that regroupments of this kind are possible without mutual condemnation.

Lukács: Yes, you see, I might here again draw attention to a case of 'this I don't know'. I cannot remember for certain whether we have already spoken of it in these conversations, I believe we have. It pertains to the general ontological characteristics of any decision, I believe, that never in the course of human development has a decision yet been made in full knowledge of all subjective and objective factors involved. And in this case, in the complicated conditions of the present time, the percentage of elements not mastered in thought is naturally extremely high, higher perhaps than it often was earlier. Let us not forget that this is in no way an ontologically new situation: it is in fact the situation of any action whatsover. And one sees retrospectively from history that people very often acted correctly on the basis of a completely false ideology. To start with quite a significant example, the voyage from Athens to Alexandria used to be guided by Ptolemaic astronomy, and yet people arrived very nicely in Alexandria and then travelled back to Athens, even though the theoretical basis of their entire movement was false. We must always keep this structure of human action in view, and understand that there are situations in which it is necessary to act, irrespective of how much we know. If I wander into a wood in a fog, I must attempt to get back home. To say that I should sit down and wait until there is a good map of that part of the Earth which I have wandered into would be ridiculous. By that time I would certainly have died of hunger. Whether I find the correct way by trial and error is another question. But trial and error is still always better than simply waiting for a complete map. The example is very crude, but I believe you will understand what I mean by it. I am not saying however that a young person today who is excited about colonialism and enthusiastically supports the uprising of the oppressed people should travel immediately to Somalia and organize an armed insurrection.

Abendroth: It is necessary to stress this last remark, for given the present stagnation of the struggles in the highly developed countries of industrial capitalism, the activism of the young generation leads very easily to false identifications. Action in these colonial countries, or better neo-colonial countries, is absolutely necessary, and solidarity with it is also indispensable, but the most important task of the young critical intellectuals must be solved in their own countries.

Lukács: Yes, this is what I believe, only it is the task of clear-sighted people in the West to give these impatient young people a rational guideline and show them that they can be of greater use to the movement in another way than by blind activism.

I witnessed the rise of fascism in Germany and I know very well that very many young people at that time adhered to fascism out of a sincere indignation at the capitalist system. Impatience, together with the historically conditioned inability of the Communist Party to change German society and development, has frequently driven decent young people into the fascist camp. We should not forget that now, and we should attempt to do the best we can to channel this energy in a direction where it can be of real use. A problem that naturally arises in this connection, and which we should also speak about, is that the mere usefulness or the mere tactical correctness of a decision is not sufficient to arouse in young people the enthusiasm which is required for practical action. The weakness of the left movements was, and in general still is, that they are not sufficiently capable of arousing this enthusiasm.

Modern practicalism, neo-positivism, behaviourism and so on gives rise to a practical tendency which even people who are generally above it concede to in a certain sense. They believe then in fact that practical activity consists solely in correct or false tactical lines of one kind or another. It is clearly the case, however, that every movement which has really achieved something has obtained the enthusiasm which made it effective from its historical perspective, not from slogans. It is interesting that even if you consider the historical operation of fascism, it was not so much mere demagogic slogans, but rather the large-scale perspectives which they contained, even if these were objectively historically false, which in the beginning aroused enthusiasm for Hitler. We cannot escape from this social dilemma that enthusiasm can only be aroused on the basis of a perspective. It is only with such a perspective that the person in question sees how his own personal life will also be changed. An *ad hominem* perspective is needed to arouse enthusiasm in someone. The great weakness of the present left movement the world over is that we are not yet in a position to develop the corresponding enthusiasm for our perspectives. This is also true for the reform movements in the socialist countries. We must understand our limitations and our errors very clearly, if we are to be in a position to do anything about this.

Abendroth: A great part of this consists in our not having developed the perspectives ourselves. The danger hence arises that the place of real perspectives is taken by sham perspectives or mere resignation. This is very clear in the example which we began to deal with here, the example of the confrontation between the developing subjectivity of the societies of the former colonial and backward countries, which had previously been degraded to objects, and the unified world of capitalist industrialism. The vital process which is now taking place in all these countries provides large sections of the young generation, who are becoming critical and tending towards the left, with a directly illuminating perspective. As a consequence of this the tendency arises to quite simply forget the possibility of their own role as subjects and to identify with the subjective tasks of the colonial revolution movement in such a way that they no longer see and no longer recognize that the first task of the young activist intelligentsia and the workers of the late-capitalist states must be accomplished in their own countries. Mere acclamation of the colonial revolution by the young intellectuals in the capitalist states is not the same as their own praxis. Rather, if they do not change the balance of power there or do not effectively hinder the intervention of the imperialist states, it is objectively only resignation in the form of sham activity. This is the negative side of Fanon's great effect on the young generation in the U.S.A. and the Federal Republic, which we are now witnessing. We must help here by explaining to this young generation that the most favourable perspective, also from the standpoint of the movements in the countries oppressed by late capitalism, is the struggle for socialism and democracy in the late-capitalist industrial countries, in these highly industrialized societies themselves, for a highly industrialized socialist society would be the most effective source of aid for the under-developed nations.

Holz: Yes, now we are faced with the situation that the entire field of science in the Western world is dominated by a type of descriptive methodology which is not suited to pointing out perspectives but rather remains fixated, so to speak, to that which it registers and records. This problem of neo-positivism arises not only in the logical and philosophical sphere, but also in the social sciences.

Lukács: The essence of the matter is the attempt, which we have already spoken of, to eliminate all ontology, to achieve the elimination of any kind of being from human praxis. Now it is possible for correct action to be carried out with a false theory, as we have already spoken about earlier, and this provides a basis for neo-positivism. It is interesting that the closer modern scientific development comes to real economic practice, for example, when a labour process is perfected by technology, the more the question whether the theoretical basis of the laws of physics and chemistry that are employed is correct or incorrect, in the sense of natural science as a whole, simply vanishes. One can possibly manipulate the world adequately, in a technological sense, on the basis of the most false theory, as in my earlier example of the ship voyage in the ancient world. Pragmatism stresses that what is successful is also true, although this thesis of pragmatism is untrue in a broader sense, not in the directly practical sense, and proves itself to be so. But the theoretical meaning of the whole then remains obscure. There can no longer be any consideration of anything beyond the existing social relations.

We are not yet carrying out this broad criticism of the neopositivist conception. The consequence of this is that every manipulative division of labour, even if it is in a certain sense necessary, as for example the separation of individual disciplines in science, produces what I would see as ontological barriers within reality. If for example a bio-physiologist makes particular bio-physiological investigations, he pays no attention at all to the rest of the organism's development. It is characteristic how a new drug is often produced which a short time later becomes notorious for its harmful side-effects on the organism. If we consider things from a neo-positivist point of view, this is simply inevitable. In investigation X only certain effects were investigated, then investigation Y takes place completely independently, and these really harmful effects emerge. Our neo-positivist is not at all troubled by the fact that both useful and harmful effects involve the same organism and the organism in fact dies, which seems to me to be an example of a most inconvenient ontological truth. In the neo-positivist's opinion, this belongs to neither series of investigation, X or Y. To return to our problem, in just the same way it is impossible to separate ontologically political, economic and personal decisions, etc. Ontologically, it is the same student who is for the oppressed nations, enthusiastically supports the backward peoples, and travels to Africa. The enthusiasm and the voyage to Africa may be separable from one another from the neo-positivist point of view, but ontologically they belong together, they take place in the same person. This has the important result for us that we are not at the present time in a position to relate the internal problems of the human personality, what would be the area of ethics, to the external social activity of the people in question.

Aristotle was a great ethical genius in this respect, for if you consider the question of the Aristotelian mean in the field of ethics, it is always a question of the concrete mean between social alternatives, and always with the double criterion that, on the one hand, it is useful for action, and on the other hand, that it promotes rather than inhibits the development of the personality. If Aristotle sought the mean between courage and cowardice, or between profligacy and miserliness, he always sought a point where both in external behaviour, and in the internal development of the person in question, the overcoming of extremes would lead to a development of the personality. Here again we have a model which should prevent a false differentiation, such as is found in neo-positivism. With this way of posing the question we can, on the one hand, prevent neo-positivism from hindering the genuinely left, genuinely progressive tendencies. On the other hand we can offer help to all those tendencies which are trying to solve an existential problem from a serious ideological standpoint. The beginnings of this are present in the still very diverse ways in which the religious need is satisfied, even if in the form of an illusory solution, a false ideology. It is on the other hand no accident that neo-positivism hastens to support this illusory subjectivism by its denial of the existence of ontological problems. For the old religious ontology broke down centuries ago. There is no one left today who believes in this ontology. On the other hand, the acceptance of that new ontology which we have finally come to speak of would lead to a demolition of the religious need and to the understanding that it leads nowhere. That is why the mere denial of the ontological standpoint, on the grounds that it is allegedly irrational and unphilosophical, is objectively of great help for all these illusory religious tendencies. I believe, if I may express myself in a rather paradoxical way, that just as Thomas Aquinas, at a certain stage of feudal development, managed to summarize all ideological requirements in a unitary system—by unifying ontology, religion and ethics—so neo-positivism, Carnap for example, plays the role of Thomas Aquinas for contemporary culture. This is naturally not pleasant for the neo-positivists to hear. It seems to me however that it is our duty to state this, and by stating it to really settle accounts with neo-positivism.

Holz: In this sense neo-positivism seems in your opinion to embody only the negative sides of Thomas's *Summa*. But did not Thomas also have his positive sides? And does Carnap really have the same importance for the ideology of late-capitalist industrial society as Thomas had for the high Middle Ages? This seems to me to be an over-estimation.

Lukács: I would of course concede this. In comparing the two, I did not mean to compare them as thinkers, but rather the social function that they performed. You should not forget that every great and influential philosophical system at one time fulfilled very important social functions. To take a positive example, Rousseauism had a very important and positive social function in the French Revolution. It is only in this sense that I would like to compare the social functions of Thomas Aquinas and Carnap.

Holz: It is interesting in this connection that a definite neo-positivist influence can even be traced in Marxist philosophy in the most recent period. I am not thinking only of the influence of Carnap on the sociology, linguistics, natural science and epistemology of many socialist states—an indirect one—but also of certain influences that can be seen for example in the cybernetic theory of George Klaus, which are basically neo-positivist in nature.

It seems to me that since neo-positivism proceeds from an absolutely non-ontological perspective and since the penetration of neo-positivist theorems can be linked with a disintegration of Marxist theory, the question of the unity of the social and historical process is thereby dissolved.

Lukács: I agree with you there. I would however like to stress at this point that the great break between Lenin and Stalin consisted precisely in that in Stalin's philosophy—if I may call it that—the temporary tactical decision of practical politics plays the primary role, so that the general theory sinks into being a trimming, a superstructure, an embellishment, which no longer has any influence on the tactical decision.

Holz: This has not been much better in the post-Stalin period. On the contrary, I would say that with Stalin, despite all the phenomena of alienation, there were occasionally more remnants of a theoretical basis of practical decisions than in many changes of the most recent era.

Lukács: Yes, that may be. I would, however, like to return here for one moment to the problem of Stalinism. With Stalin the attempt to found socialist decisions theoretically took a manipulative turn, in contrast to the period of Marx and Lenin. As far as overcoming the Stalin period is concerned, we are still at the stage in which the most gross errors of Stalinism are still being overcome with Stalin's methods. We have not yet reached the point at which Stalin's methods themselves are being overcome. And this neo-positivist tendency in present-day Marxism is related to the predominance of tactics over theoretical principles. It is inevitable that in certain theoretical matters we are verging on neo-positivism. This is not only a scientific flattening, a distortion of Marxism, but also a practical constraint on the ideological influence of the ideas of socialism in the world today. In the most difficult times of civil war and hunger the mere existence of the soviet socialist republic aroused the enthusiasm of wide circles in the West, precisely because many people felt: here they are fighting for something that involves the most basic problems of their own existence, they are striving to put an end to the questionable status of human existence under capitalism. The brutal manipulation of the Stalin period wiped away these expectations. The alleviation and technical refinement of this manipulation could not re-establish the lost enthusiasm, and cannot do so, until a break is made with manipulation—the refined as well as the brutal kind.

The rise of a new man is a perspective that can arouse international enthusiasm. The mere prospect of a rising standard of living can by itself certainly not do so—though I don't underestimate the practical importance of this in the socialist countries. No one will be converted to socialism by the perspective of owning a car, especially if he already has one under capitalism.

Only if praxis reassumes that form which it had with Marx and Lenin will this negative influence be broken. Just consider how Lenin, in his polemic against Bukharin in the course of the trade-union debate, introduced into the discussion the category of totality, although he knew quite well, and stressed it, that we can never fully know the totality of determinations. If you consider on the other hand Adorno's descriptive aphorism, that the untruth is the whole, you see how through this way of posing the problem the momentary practical decision is made into an absolute measure of our standpoint. If the single great question in Germany today, for example, really is whether Brandt or Erhard can form a grand coalition or not, then you will never find a way for decent young people to discover in such questions the problem of their own life. This requires posing a quite different question about German destiny, although one can certainly discuss the merits and demerits of the grand coalition within this perspective. I believe it is clear to you what I mean here, and that we are faced here with a general feature of politics, a general feature of economic manipulation. It would be a wonder if this did not show itself in ideology. It is also very interesting as regards the most recent ideological development that the resistance to this manipulative tendency is growing and that on this account neo-positivism is undoubtedly no longer so unquestionably prevalent as it was for example only a few years ago.